Why Live?

THE BEAUTIFUL AND PAINFUL MESS OF LEARNING TO LOVE LIFE

Faolan Sugarman-Lash

I wrote this book to the best of my memory, but as we all know memory can be a fickle thing. Some names and identifying details have been changed without interfering with the integrity of truth. In all cases, make your own judgments in your life and do not make decisions solely based on the words I wrote about mine.

Published by Sow Flow Publishing
sowflow.co

First Edition 2022
Paperback: 979-8-9852916-0-5
Hardcover: 979-8-9852916-1-2
Ebook: 979-8-9852916-2-9

Library of Congress Control Number: 2021924346

Book and Cover Designed by Renée Stevens
Edited by Shaina Clingempeel

DEDICATION

To Life:
Thank you for the gifts of breathing, feeling,
knowing, loving, and living.

To My Sisters:
Thank you for melting the ice covering my heart.

To You:
Thank you for being alive. You matter.
You are here for a reason.

TABLE OF CONTENTS

INTRODUCTION

"Do you think trees wonder why they're alive?"
- ME

If you have ever wondered why you're alive or, like me, wanted to die, then this book is for you. This mission is for you. As long as there is one person who doesn't want to live, and when I say "live" I mean Thoreau-marrow-sucking-YARP living, then this book matters, this effort matters, we matter, because we are here to LIVE, not simply exist.

The dream: Each of us living as our true selves, wanting and experiencing every second of our lives, beauty, pain, mediocrity, and wonder included.

Truth be told, we're a long way from this utopia. I don't want to prattle off statistics to you about high suicide, depression, and addiction rates. I don't want to even accept that people do kill themselves, whether it be slowly, day-by-day, moment-to-moment slippage or all at once. I don't want to talk about any of this because it hurts. It hurts to feel the pain of knowing people don't want to live and to have known that pain myself. It hurts to write about the pain and to stand up for healing it...

But it is necessary work for me because in my pain lies my purpose. We are all intimate with the existential pain of being alive and thus we all have a source to draw from. Deep inside our pain, we hold unique truths that only we can offer the world. We have our own stories to share using our own art forms, and maybe that's what it means to be human.

Hundreds of people have shared their life stories with me, and I have never been bored. Each of us carries a whole human soul ripe with spectrums of emotions, thoughts, goals, expectations, and traumas. Because we're autonomous beings, we all face the same question: "Why Live?"

This question comes in two forms. When I'm experiencing depression, it haunts me. When I'm fully present to life with joy and gratitude, it piques my curiosity and becomes a beacon on the horizon. In my story you will see how this question transforms from darkness into light.

This book is a tale of suffering and trauma, of failure and mistakes, and of healing, love, and hope. This book is my answer to the question that has brought me tears of pain and tears of joy.

In my story, I hope that you may see your own. As I was lost, so you may be. As I found my answer, you will assuredly find yours. Do not lose hope.

May you find your answer mirrored in the pages of my story and may you live as only you can, as you.

Let curiosity guide you to ever-present light.

Welcome, and enjoy.

This is: *Why Live?*

A GLOSSARY OF TERMS

In my book, I define words for myself because I believe that language is a flowing and evolving set of tools used to best communicate our experiences to each other, not a rigid framework. It's important that you know my definitions of the following terms:

"Life" vs "life" - "Life" with a capital "L" is the constant flowing evolution that always has been and always will be. "life" with a lower-case "l" is an individual being's experience of Life, as in yours or mine.

Reality - Directly experiencing the full spectrum of Life as a whole and one's life.

Fantasy - Where reality is what is, fantasy is what might be or what has been; ie. not real.

Suffering - Suffering is escaping from reality into fantasy to escape pain.

Pain - Pain is anything that hurts our hearts.

Trauma - Trauma is pain that we haven't healed from but that is still inside us and negatively affects how we live.

Truth - That which resonates with the deepest parts of our being.

God/Universe/Divine etc - That which makes us experience awe. The word we use isn't important, the feeling is. In my book God is a placeholder word but any will do.

God vs Gods - God (or any other word) is the overall experience of awe and majesty of Life. Gods are personal; we each have our own subjective experience of Life, so we each have our own personal feeling of Godliness or the Divine.

"One is compelled to recognize that all these imprecise words are kind of attempts made by us all to get to something, which is real and which lives behind the words... It seems to me that the artist's struggle for his integrity, is a kind of metaphor... for the struggle, which is universal and daily, of all human beings on the face of this terrifying globe to get to become human beings...

What is important... is that you must find some way of using this [pain] to connect you with everyone else alive. This is all you have to do it with. You must understand that your pain is trivial except insofar as you can use it to connect with other people's pain; and insofar as you can do that with your pain, you can be released from it; and then hopefully, it works the other way around, too. Insofar as I can tell you what it's like to suffer, perhaps you can suffer less..."

– JAMES BALDWIN

-PRELUDE-
THE STORY BEGINS

When the messiah comes and you hold a sapling
in your hands, first plant the sapling and then go
to greet the messiah.
— A JEWISH PROVERB

On New Year's Eve 2020, I drove 16 hours in one day from Atlanta, Georgia to my hometown of Richmond, Massachusetts. While driving, I listened to Richard Powers' novel *The Overstory*. By the time I arrived home at 11 pm, I had listened to the whole book. For those who haven't read his book, it is a reminder of reality in the face of the climate crisis. At the end of his book, I was faced with a dismal question: If the odds that we can save our planet and our species are low, then what's the point of living?

The next morning, on New Year's Day, I woke up at 3:27 in the morning struck by epiphany. I bolted up in my bed and for the next three hours wrote what would become the first real outline for this book. I wrote of the stark reality my generation faces as we look toward the future. I wrote of trauma and healing. I wrote of the beauty and pain that life holds. I wrote of hopeful things, and I wrote of challenging things.

This book came to me like striking gold just as my pick-axe wore out. When I was nearing the end of my hope, this book came to save me. I share it with you so that it might bring to you that which it has brought to me: A profound love for Life, mine and ours, painful and beautiful.

I first read the quote at the beginning of this chapter in *The Overstory*. After looking into it more, I found that it's a Jewish saying. This quote, more than most, has driven the creation of my book. To me, it means that we each have a gift to give and that before we die it is our job to give it. By giving our deepest gifts, we become our truest selves.
May you be **You** for the sake of **All**.

In my story there are seven steps. Each step corresponds to one part of my book but, like parts of a story, these steps build on each other. Beyond the seven steps, you are free to be, do, or create anything that calls to you but remember that you must live as yourself and no one else. This requires returning to each step many times along your path. The journey is never done, but as you walk your path, you will find freedom, fulfillment, and meaning.

First, become aware.
Second, accept yourself.
Third, awaken to Life.
Fourth, align inside with out.
Fifth, find awe.
Sixth, come alive.
Seventh, create your Art.

Let the story begin.

PART 1
THE FOG DESCENDS

AWARENESS

"

A boy at the beginning of a story has no way
of knowing that the story has begun.

"

— ERIN MORGENSTERN

-1-

TRAUMA AND SUFFERING

*"Secrets of the heart are different. They are private
and painful, and we want nothing more than to
hide them from the world. They do not swell and
press against the mouth. They live in the heart, and
the longer they are kept, the heavier they become.
Teccam claims it is better to have a mouthful of
poison than a secret of the heart. Any fool will spit
out poison, he says, but we hoard these painful
treasures. We swallow hard against them every
day, forcing them deep inside us. There they sit,
growing heavier, festering. Given enough time, they
cannot help but crush the heart that holds them."*
— PATRICK ROTHFUSS

We all are traumatized as children from the natural pain
of life. Children cannot heal their pain, so they hold it inside without awareness. Eventually, we become aware of
that childhood trauma, and it is still overwhelming, so we
ignore it at all costs. This makes us suffer. In order to heal,
you must first find not only awareness, but acceptance
of your suffering and unresolved trauma. To resolve your
trauma, you must own your trauma.

—⟩⟩⟩⟩⟩—

My parents were young when they had me. My mom was 19 and my dad was 22. They separated when I was 8 months old. I don't have any memories of being a family, but I do have a photo from when I was a baby. In it, my parents are smiling and holding me in their arms. Even as I write about it, tears fill my eyes... Tears always come when I think about my parents being together.

My earliest memory is a painful one. I sat at the bottom of a staircase, looking up at my mom sitting on the steps. It was dark outside and gloomy in the house. She held a cordless home phone to her ear and tears spilled from her eyes. I was young enough to be in tune with her emotions without having words for them. I felt her pain but didn't understand it. She was on the phone with my dad. She yelled into the receiver, hung up, and her tears returned.

This memory may or may not be accurate. It may be a combination of memories or a distortion. Whatever the case, it was real for me. Whether it actually happened as I remember is irrelevant. The memory still exists in my head, heart, and soul. This memory represented what made me lose my ability to love, feel loved, and understand love, but was only a piece of my childhood trauma.

We almost all experience trauma in our childhoods. Our trauma stems from an experience of pain that we aren't able to understand or heal from as a child. For me, it was the excruciating pain of watching my parents fight without knowing why. I think that at one point they earnestly loved each other, but soon after I was born that love transformed into anger, fear, doubt, shame, and hurt. They both felt rejected, unseen, unloved. I was in the middle of it, holding space in the tension.

No parent wants their children to experience this kind of trauma, but many children do. We are imperfect humans, parents included, and things rarely, if ever, go according to plan. But, that's what it means to be alive and so we must make do with what we're given.

When I was about 4, I was in bed with my wind-up teddy bear for bedtime. My mom wound up my bear, who played a lullaby. Then, my mom began to sing along. As I listened to her sing and to the sounds of my teddy bear, I drifted off to sleep. Right before I entered dreamland, I heard her say, "I love you." I remember hearing it but not feeling it.

I never doubted that I was loved, but I didn't understand how to feel that love. It was abstract. I received love into an empty void of blackness. Love came to me, withered, and then died. As a child, I couldn't understand love, couldn't feel it. I heard my mom's words but couldn't accept them because I believed I was the cause of her pain and thus couldn't be worthy of love.

As a child, I had an unformed and unconscious thought that because I was born my parents experienced pain. I blamed myself for their tension, tears, and unresolved trauma. I put so much pressure on myself to hold the tension between my parents in the hope that they wouldn't have to hurt so much. It was this, more than anything, that caused my heart wound.

At the time, I didn't have the capacity to understand my pain, let alone feel it, let alone heal it... so I didn't. Instead, I became an expert middleman, a contortionist of sorts who held space for mother and father without letting myself enjoy life. I didn't know that my parent's emotions weren't my responsibility and thought that it was my job to make them happy. This was the trauma, the thorn inside me that would control my life for decades to come. But I couldn't do anything about it, so I hid it away inside myself, transformed it into a secret inner pain and, in doing so, freed myself to enjoy being a child.

Despite hiding it inside, there were moments when it came back to me suddenly and without desire. Any question from one side of my family about the other brought the tension back, made me answer blithely. In those moments, I lived to please, to ease, and to comfort. I lost myself in the fear of retaliation. I couldn't bear to see my parents in pain and so I protected them from each other. This was challenging, but only came in bursts, sudden and bright, then gone with the wind. Mostly, I have fond memories of my childhood.

For the first 11 years of my life, I played pretend games in the forest and learned to love books and other worlds. I fell into Pokémon and Magic cards and Dungeons and Dragons. I managed to enjoy life by escaping into fantasy worlds. This worked for a while, but eventually, inevitably the darkness came.

When I was 11, I transferred to a public middle school from a small private one. It wasn't an easy transition. I was called The Great Wall of China because I was the only Asian boy on my middle school soccer team. I was laughed at for having the dandruff in my hair. Despite my passion for learning and school, I grew resentful and jealous of the "normal" and "cool" kids. I watched them joke and play by bullying each other and I thought that I could join in, that perhaps by becoming someone else, I could let go of the pain of rejection. I learned not to share about my nerdy hobbies and to talk like others talked. I lost track of my passions in the flurry of posturing that was middle school. My romantic pursuits didn't go much better.

I was rejected by every girl I asked out and each rejection reinforced the false narrative that I had been the cause of my parents' pain, unwanted, and unworthy of being loved... or alive. Each time I was teased or rejected, my fears and unworthiness layered on top of my trauma, hiding it deeper inside me. I lost more of my true self each day and began to blend in. I couldn't be myself, so I became someone else, someone perfectly suited to external validation. I became an automaton that excelled at "succeeding" but forfeited the ability to be myself or feel alive.

I slipped into suffering and an utterly numb denial of myself and reality. I escaped taking responsibility for my life by letting other people set my path and my priorities. I didn't try to solve my problems because they overwhelmed me. I didn't try to understand my problems because everyone around me assumed that I had different, more important ones. The adults in my life didn't seem to worry about my self-worth or my hidden traumas because I didn't tell them. Instead, they worried about my grades and my "future."

The problem with that was that pain is in the present and must be engaged in the present. I learned to live for an unnamed future, impossible fantasies of what laid beyond the numbness. I escaped my current suffering by looking into fantasies of life. "Good grades would let me escape this numbness, right?" "College will be better, right?" I was never present.

I don't blame my parents or family or teachers for guiding me into the future and into fantasies. It's what people in America are conditioned to do. From birth, we are asked what we want to be when we grow up, not who we are. Suffering perpetuates suffering.

People watched me and saw that I was achieving above average signs of "success." I got good grades, was liked by my teachers, and seemed to have decent friends. They saw me playing soccer games and Magic tournaments. They saw me reading and having sleepovers. From the outside, I looked alright, successful even. However, external, societally defined, "success" did not equate to my internal health. On the inside, I was in a numb turmoil, like a colorless molasses whirlpool dragging me down.

Middle school taught me to be a phenomenal actor. I learned to hide my pain under external "success" and I looked for the things that people wanted to see me do.

I worked hard to do those things, not only to maintain the external facade of my happiness, but especially to maintain the inner one. I wasn't just deceiving those around me, but myself. The busier I kept myself, the less I had to look within. I stayed busy to avoid myself and I was excellent at it.

I excelled in school, made many surface-level friends, and gently sucked up to teachers in ways they wouldn't expect. I always had a smile on my face even when I was suffering inside. As I practiced faking life, it became second nature and, eventually, it was so easy to do that I didn't try anymore. I had become a robot more suited to being a cog than a person. Only one thing still made me come alive: Learning... And even that would crumble away.

In my sophomore year of high school, I was in a class that I actually liked. We read books about dystopias and philosophy. It was interesting, engaging, and let me wonder at life. I loved the books we read, books like *Catch 22*, *The Great Gatsby*, and *Revolutionary Road*. Reading about concepts that pushed my brain, made me question myself, question my pain. I could have come awake in that class, but it was not meant to be. In fact, that class was the straw that broke my back, that took away my last care for school.

One day in class, one of my teachers said that I was sexist because I agreed with the male philosopher's opinion, not the female's. I remember feeling snuffed out, like a candle 'neath a metal thimble. To be named a sexist by a teacher in front of everyone in the only class I actually cared about... And for something so ridiculous... It was too much for me and I broke. After that, I couldn't bring myself to care. It was preposterous. I felt attacked by the very person I should be able to trust. I never read another assigned book for all of high school.

Before this moment, some part of me cared about what I was learning, about growing. I was interested and invested in life, to a small degree. Even if I wasn't being my true and whole self, I still cared about things. I was curious still. After that moment, it was as if the wind didn't blow. My sails couldn't find the strength to carry me anymore. Instead of giving my own effort, I started to cheat efficiently during study hall. I completely lost faith and stopped living to learn and learned to live without living at all.

Because I had tried hard in school when younger, I had earned a brand as a "good kid" or a "bright student." That brand carried me through school because teachers thought that I was smart, that I cared. Many people don't have this brand and flunk out. I was lucky. Many suffering adolescents aren't given any time of day because they don't have this branding. I was really no different than the people who skipped class to smoke cigarettes outside. I sat in class and let words wash over me without meaning. We were all suffering; I was simply branded as a "good student" and so I passed by unnoticed. I conformed instead of rebelled, shrinking into a numb life.

High school was the prime of suffering in my life. I was so detached from reality that I didn't truly engage with life.

The emphasis here is on the word "truly." In classes I made jokes with friends, asked questions, and did my homework. On the soccer team, I ran just as many laps as others. In track, I was even the MVP for a season. But despite these "efforts," I felt empty. Despite doing what others did, I felt directionless.

I remember the feeling of running around the soccer field. I watched as my friends pushed themselves and ran harder than I ever could. They cared and it showed. Some numbed part of me might have cared, too, but I was disconnected, numb to the emotions required to give life my all. When I say "truly" engage, I'm talking about the enthusiasm, the emphasis, the exclamation mark on life. I didn't have those things, I only floated.

With one exception, everything I did in high school, I was numb to. The only thing that somehow escaped my numbness was Magic: The Gathering. Magic is a card game mostly played by adults. You might imagine a somewhat overweight man who doesn't smell so good in a backpack. This would be accurate for some people, but not all. The Magic community was expansive, beyond stereotype. Some players were college students, professors, technology executives, or kids like me. The common trend between all the players was the love of the game. For me, Magic was everything. I poured my heart into that game for almost 10 years. It was the only thing I wanted to talk about.

My dream was to be a professional Magic player, but I never believed in myself. I wanted it more than anything but didn't have the courage or ability to make it happen. Because I learned from a young age to fit in, hold space, and conform, I wasn't able to break out of my self-imposed cage and follow my dreams. My trauma still controlled my capacity, like a numbing agent on my passions. I didn't know this at the time, but in order to be our best selves, we must let go of our fear and accept our traumas and our pains. Because I held them so tightly, I limited myself and only left room for escape from myself.

Everything else I did during high school was to avoid what I stored deep inside myself. I kept myself comfortable and disengaged from reality by escaping into distractions like porn, video games, and TV. I was suffering in numbness and didn't know it. Everything I did was harder than it should be. I had headaches for no reason, and I couldn't think straight most of the time. I was making myself depressed by avoiding my pain and trauma. Stuck in suffering, I was unable to experience pain and thus unable to experience real joy...

By avoiding my trauma, I let myself become someone completely formed by external forces, losing access to my dreams, myself, and my true potential. Because I was afraid to feel my pain, I made myself suffer. It was more comfortable for me to live my life waiting to die than it was to work through my trauma and pain. Spiritual depression incarnated: Waiting to die with no awareness at all.

Despite everything, even in the darkest times the light shines through. These moments are what lead us to the greater light. They are but glimpses of something greater, something beyond. They are ephemeral and gossamer, as if butterfly wings on the wind. We cannot hold onto them for we are still lost in the writhing, numbing battle with darkness, but we may enjoy their respite and their light... We may appreciate the moments of light and be grateful, for they will show us the way through the darkness.

-2-

FLICKERS OF LIGHT

"In the end, truth will out."
– SHAKESPEARE

Soon after I got my license, I was driving down a winding road in my grandparents' car. It was summer and my music blared. A song came on that I didn't want to listen to, so I pulled out my phone and changed it. As the next song began, I heard a screeching sound from outside my car. I threw my phone down and my stomach seemed to rise into my throat. I was sliding against the guardrail. I grabbed the wheel and jerked myself back into the road.

My head felt like it had been thrown into a freezing lake. Thoughts came to me like juxtaposing knights riding into a joust. "My grandparents are going to kill me!" "Thank God I'm alive." Then, down the hill..."What should I do?"

The answer came quickly. I realized that my only choice was to tell the truth and accept responsibility for my mistake. Because of my trauma I was afraid that I would be rejected by my grandparents and that I would lose their love for what I had done, but what happened was the opposite. When I told them the truth, they didn't care at all about the car and were just glad that I was alive.

In retrospect it seems obvious that their priority would be my safety, but at the time I had spent so many years conditioning myself to conform, keep the peace, and be small that I didn't believe I could be loved even as I failed. I thought that failure to maintain the equilibrium would inevitably lead to abandonment. My grandparents were the first people to show me that their love for me was greater than any mistake I could make. Their love was unconditional.

Because I let myself be vulnerable, I gave them the chance to show me unconditional love. Without vulnerability, we cannot receive authentic and unconditional love. By opening myself, I opened the doors to the love that had been there all along. Only in retrospect do I see the significance of that moment. It was my first taste of opening to love by sharing my Truth.

Honesty became my first authentic core value. Over the years, honesty has evolved into greater values like Integrity, Truth, and Authenticity. Through honesty and vulnerability, I began my journey into the light from the darkness. I had a long way to go but this was the moment that foreshadowed what was yet to come. Beyond my grandparents' forgiveness and acceptance of me, two other people showed me the light of unconditional love.

My half-sisters, Eliya and Simona, were born when I was 15 and 13 respectively. As I suffered in my colorless fog, they were born into the world with the fresh and vibrant view of children. Just as love was lost to me, it was all they had. They saw vibrance where I saw decay. They were Life embodied, and they may have saved mine.

My sisters loved me fully, with their entire beings in a different way than a parent loves their child. My sisters didn't expect me to be any certain way or do any certain thing, they just loved me for who I was. They didn't want me to get good grades or do the dishes. They didn't care that I was hiding my pain or that I was escaping from reality. They saw me as children see: Without expectations and judgment.

They saw my essence clearly and they loved me for me.

Their unconditional love for me shone like fiery rays of light on my dark, shadowed shell, piercing holes in my defenses. Their love pierced not like a needle pierces or a sword pricks. It pierced like the sun pierces the night, all-encompassing and new. In the midst of their love, I still suffered, but gained hope and light. By loving me for me, they began my healing process. Without them, I might still be surrounded in defenses, incapable of love.

True, consistent, unconditional love and acceptance can break the barriers of pain, suffering, and self-loathing. My grandparents and my sisters showed me that I had value not because of what I produced but because I existed. They validated my life in a way that I couldn't do for myself and that I couldn't hear from my parents because of my trauma. They showed me that I mattered and shone the first lights on my darkness. The door to healing, awareness, and self-acceptance creaked ever so slightly open but still sat behind monsters, demons, and dragons. My journey began without me even knowing. I still had a lot to learn.

-3-

HURT PEOPLE HURT PEOPLE

"When another person makes you suffer, it is because he suffers deeply within himself, and his suffering is spilling over. He does not need punishment; he needs help. That's the message he is sending."
– THICH NHAT HANH

After high school, I chose between two colleges. One was 2 hours from my hometown by car and the other was 7 hours by plane. Subconsciously I knew which decision I needed to make but was scared to commit to moving across the country. Eventually, I made the choice and flew across the country to begin my college education at Santa Clara University.

If you had asked me when I was 18 why I was going to college, I would have told you some bullshit answer about saving the world or learning how to start businesses. The reality was that I had no idea why. I went because everyone else around me was going but I had no real "Why."

My first year in college went by in somewhat of a blur beneath the fog of my spiritual depression. I made new friends, drank too much for the first, second, and twelfth time, got good grades in classes I didn't really care about, and thought about dropping out every day. Looking back now, I didn't really care about anything I was doing, and it showed. I continued to be an automaton, going along with what was expected of me. One important decision changed the trajectory of my life.

At the end of my first year, I applied to be an orientation leader and was accepted, which meant that every week, I would help 1,500 incoming first-years get oriented to college. Looking back, this job came at a perfect time because it pushed me way outside my comfort zone and showed me my potential.

For the first 19 years of my life, I felt completely rejected by society and conformed to what was expected of me. This job, which encouraged us to be goofy, over the top, and enthusiastic, was the exact opposite. Instead of hiding myself and going with the flow, I was paid to scream at the top of my lungs, wear glitter and bright clothes, and dance for ten minutes in front of over a thousand students. It was the perfect way to get me out of my shell and into a newer, more confident version of myself.

The job was so much fun. We woke up at 5 am, chugged Red Bulls, and paraded through the hallways blaring *Thunderstruck* into the dark morning fog. We took that energy and brought it to the new students. We worked from before sunrise to after sunset talking to, walking around with, and teaching new students. It was wonderfully uncomfortable and with the discomfort came a new joy I hadn't experienced before. I hadn't ever pushed myself beyond my comfort zone for the sake of another person. This job inspired me to strive for more than I had been before in order to serve the new students.

I wanted to be more, to serve better but didn't know who to become so I tried new personalities on. I was allowed to be anyone as long as I was enthusiastic and compassionate, so I experimented with myself. I practiced being outgoing, confident, and assertive. I practiced being quiet, composed, and reserved. I yelled at the top of my lungs and found silent spots to read. It was the first time I felt able to play around with who I showed the world and it freed me to try living life my own way, without conforming to anyone's expectations of me.

When everyone else on the team went to lunch or hung out together, I brought my hammock to a secret spot on campus and napped or read books. When other people on the team gossiped and made drama, I stepped back. When the rest of the team drank, I drank, too. It was a boisterous summer with occasional pauses for quiet and peace.

We made trips to San Francisco and Big Sur on the weekends. We hiked and played music. We drank and sat on rooftops laughing late into the night. When we weren't at work, we were free to enjoy our time. However, when we were at work, we worked hard to serve the new students.

With hundreds of new students meeting, the shy ones often backed into the shadows. I loved to work them out of their shells just as much as I loved to dance with the ones who were excited to dance. Being of service to people in a way I enjoyed made this job matter for me. I was helping people come into their own and be themselves. Looking back, it was the beginning of my career as a life coach, but I had no idea.

The job started me down my path of introspection and growth. Over and over again, parents asked me to share my story: "Why did I decide to live in that dorm?" "What are my classes like?" "Did I struggle to make friends?" And over and over again I told them my story: I came to SCU because it was new and exciting and because the people were warm and friendly, my classes were mostly good, and I had quality friends.

It was in the repetition of my storytelling that I started to listen to the words I was saying. Only after telling my story a hundred times did I start to understand that I didn't really know the answers to some of their questions. I didn't know why I was at Santa Clara or who I wanted to be. As the summer went on and I found more self-awareness, my answers evolved. As my answers changed, I started to shape them into aspirations. Instead of saying "I don't know who I am, why I'm here, or where I'm going" I guessed at answers that resonated for me. I didn't know any of those things, but I was given the opportunity to guess and in that guessing I found my first taste of agency.

I started to map out my own purpose through awareness and people listened.

Because people listened to my stories, I started to believe that my story mattered and that I mattered. It was my first taste of affirmation from third party people and it fed my ego. I became confident but only on the surface. I was still suffering within. My confidence was a new kind of barrier over my deeper trauma that protected me from looking within. My story and the way I told it changed but I still wasn't drawing from my core self. I wasn't confident, but arrogant.

Arrogance is like confidence but covers deep insecurity and pain. Confidence isn't hiding anything, it's not born in shame, it's born in wholeness. Arrogance is a shameful emotion meant to dominate others in order to keep one's self safe. Because of the attention I got as an orientation leader, my arrogance blossomed and replaced my shyness. I swapped one shield for another, but still didn't heal my deeper wounds.

There's a key piece that I can't overemphasize: I was growing closer to being capable of seeing inside. Even though I was still running away from my feelings and was using arrogance as a tool to shield myself, I was actively trying new things. In high school, I very rarely tried new things and was stagnant. Because I wasn't getting out of my comfort zone, nothing I did made me feel my trauma or deal with it. In college, I started to make way more mistakes and it opened me up to actually growing.

As I shifted from shyness to arrogance, my identity changed and so did the way I interacted with the outside world. I did things that I hadn't ever done before. I started to try more things and make more mistakes. The beginning of my intentional and aware self-growth journey wasn't pretty. I messed up, hurt people, and paid the price for being a self-centered asshole. Again, it was not pretty. Eventually, I grew because I needed to, not because I wanted to.

In the fall of my sophomore year, I got a job as a community facilitator, our school's version of residential assistant. After being an orientation leader, which was fun and free, being a community facilitator was closed, restricting, and boring. I wasn't allowed to drink, go to parties, or hook up with any of the residents in the building I lived in. Guess what I did that quarter... All of the above, as much as possible. Welcome to rebellion.

After I finished my job as orientation leader, which I loved, I started a new job that I hated. In my arrogant state of being, I signed up for 7 classes in the fall and was totally dissatisfied with school. Beyond that, I was still lost in life. I added more and more wood to the fire so that I could avoid looking inside at the darkness that had started to seep out.

With my newfound arrogance, I numbed my pain not only with alcohol and porn, but by seeking external validation from women. I partied at least twice every week and sought out hookups to draw away the pain of living a life I hated. In the span of 10 weeks, I hooked up with 10 women.

My biggest regret in life so far is that I put the wellbeing of others at risk because of my own avoidance. In a dark way, it's funny because it could have gone even worse for everyone involved. The kicker that actually saved me from causing major harm to myself or others is that my porn addiction made it impossible for me to get hard with any of the women I hooked up with so I couldn't have sex. This is perhaps the only silver lining of my whole addiction. Still, because I ran from myself, I drank too much and put other people at risk.

For years, my rejections defined me, so when I was accepted by beautiful women, my ego ballooned, and I made stupid decisions. Beyond the hookups themselves, I shared stories with friends and even high fived someone while making out with a girl. I gloated and sought praise for myself because I thought I was winning at life. According to society, being *that guy* was cool... Little did I know that I was being an asshole. I started to get a reputation for being *that guy* in ways I never wanted.

One day, on a hike with two friends from orientation, I got called out. My friend told me that all the other orientation leaders were talking about me and had lost respect for me. It hurt to hear and made me acknowledge that I was being belligerent and careless with the feelings of the women I hooked up with. My arrogance fed on external validation, so when I was given Truth by an objective observer, my facade crumbled and I was left with only shame and a question: "Am I a good person?"

That question made me step back. The shame I felt made me question myself and empathize with others. From that place of empathy, I realized that I actually wasn't being a good person. Deep down, I was a good person but I wasn't acting like it.

It took me years to integrate that realization into my choices and actions. This is a theme in my book and in my life. I've had many realizations, but consistently, it's taken much longer to integrate them into my life than I expected. As you continue to read, notice how long it takes me to integrate each realization, epiphany, and lesson into my life. Remember that the healing path is not short, easy, or straight. It is a long and winding road that never ends. Have compassion and empathy for yourself as you grow and for me as you read. We are all human and we fail often at the same things we promised to never fail at again. As Alexander Pope wrote, "to err is human; to forgive, divine." I hope to never forget this.

Another friend of mine, around the same time, said that I was well-known around school as someone who only befriended women to hookup with them. I was hurt and offended by her words. I thought of myself as a good person who cared about others. Looking back, she was right.

Looking back, I hooked up with almost all of my female friends from freshman and sophomore year of college.

For a while, I hated myself for seeking out so many unhealthy flings and didn't even understand why I was doing it. I hated hurting women I genuinely cared for.

Looking back, I'm able to give myself some grace. I forgave myself for making mistakes because only through those mistakes did I learn to grow. Those mistakes catalyzed my healing journey. I saw my potential to hurt others and that my suffering caused others pain. That was the first time I really knew I needed to change.

My life was not healthy. I wasn't happy and I wasn't doing anything productive about it. On the surface, I was having fun, but I wasn't fulfilled. At a deeper level, I was broken, and that brokenness was hurting the people around me. I was covered in broken glass. Whenever anyone gave me love—hugged me—it hurt them, and it hurt me. I needed to change but I didn't yet know how to.

-4-

THE MONKEY BARS AND
THE HAMMOCK

*"If I could do anything, would it be what I'm doing
today or something different?"*
– CHRIS GUILLEBEAU

Between porn, sexless hookups, alcohol, seven classes, and 20 hours of work a week, I was effectively avoiding my pain. I overloaded myself to escape my feelings and to find external validation.

My inner story at the time was that the more women who wanted to hook up with me, the more attractive and successful I was and that with success would come feelings of love and acceptance. I was looking for meaning in external validation because if I stopped to look in the mirror, I would find a broken person. I wasn't able to slow down because, subconsciously, I was scared to let myself feel.

I want to be clear, the main issue leading to my suffering was not that I had a lot on my plate or that I was seeking external validation. Those were both stemming from a deeper root cause. At my core, my suffering stemmed from a lack of authenticity, which came from my childhood trauma and the conforming that followed. I didn't understand yet, but I was escaping from reality because I didn't know who I was. My search for external validation through hookups and my packed schedule acted as numbing agents so that I wouldn't have to go inside myself.

But, because I was overworking myself and was exhausted, my control over my emotional landscape started to slip. I was so busy that I stopped being able to repress certain feelings. The more women I hooked up with, the more my inner conscience clawed and scratched at the prison I had put it in so many years before. The more hours I put into the job I hated, the more my pain raged at me. I was starting to feel again. After years of numbing myself to life and escaping, my pain was coming out. The very defenses that I put in place became so overwhelming that they fell apart. I broke down and my pain flowed out of me in uncontrollable bursts.

The guilt of hooking up with women, the doubt about life that came with doing a job I hated, and the fear of never changing unlocked in me an ability to grow that I had been stifling for years. I began to listen to myself. I started to let myself feel emotions that challenged me in little bits and pieces. At the time, I wasn't conscious of this process, but looking back, I was learning to listen to my heart.

As the dam around my heart started to break open, all sorts of things that I had been holding poured out. I suddenly realized that I had dreams. Until that point, I never really understood that I could dream of a full and happy life.

In November of my sophomore year, I realized that I wanted to explore the world and search for myself along the way. I wanted to learn, grow, and come into the best version of myself, on my own terms. As I embraced this truth, I lit up with joy.

At the time my dream was something like this: "I'm going to drop out of college, buy a plane ticket to somewhere really cool, and find the meaning of life." It was straightforward, exciting, and naive.

Having a dream made me light up from within. Until I started to dream from the inside, I wasn't really alive. Until I allowed myself to hope from the inside, I was like a lightbulb with no light shining in it. I wasn't lit, I didn't have my spark. Once I had a dream, I lit up, my spark was there.

Still, it wasn't easy. It was new and exciting but with the burgeoning dreams came a dissonance between the life I wanted and the life I was living. I saw how my life wasn't what I wanted it to be, and I broke down.

I told one of my friends about my dream and he said, "Faolan, you can't drop out of college, that just won't work." It was as if every ounce of my excitement had been ousted from my body like a punch to the gut. I was shackled once more to my suffering.

It went something like this: *I found a seed for a beautiful tree. I showed my friend the seed and said, "Look at this beautiful tree!" My friend looked back at me and laughed because it wasn't a tree but a seed. When I looked back down at my tree-seed, it had blown away.*

Dreams are fragile when they're born. They need to be protected and nurtured before they can be shown around. Sadly, it took me years to learn this lesson. At the time, I simply didn't understand that.

So, I kept showing people my dream and after talking to many friends, family members, and mentors I convinced myself that to dream was wrong. I realized with stark clarity that it wasn't my place to think that I could escape the system of hoops set up for me from birth. Who was I to do life differently? I was just some kid. Looking back, I didn't have the courage, self-belief, and resilience that is needed to embody my dreams. I let the pressure of conforming to the opinions of others weigh me down again. In dreaming something different, I had become different, and I didn't have the tenacity to be different yet.

After losing hope in my dream, I meandered through life waiting for something to change. I was like a deflated balloon, aimlessly searching for something to blow me up again.

One night, when I was feeling exceptionally low and hopeless, I went out for a late-night stroll. I wore my earbuds and put on the song *Green Eyes*, by Coldplay. It was a cold night near the end of November, and I was bundled up. I walked past different dorms on campus and longed to sing but didn't want to wake people up, so I stayed quiet. Eventually, I found myself near some monkey bars used for exercising. I looked up at the monkey bars and climbed to the top. I sat down on the structure and looked out into the cloudy, winter night.

Suddenly, like a gunshot on a silent night, panic struck me. I came infinitely close to tears only for my heart to shut down. I felt the tears coming, my body tensing, then they would vanish, and I would go numb again. I was on a loop: Feel, ache, shut down, repeat.

I continued my emotional loop and my brain started to analyze my feelings. I wondered why I was even alive if I wasn't following my heart. With what purpose was I even living for? This was the first time I had directly asked myself these questions. I had gotten so low that I only had two options:

1. Avoid the questions and become totally numb to life, living as a dead husk... or
2. Face the questions in the hopes that I could some how find answers.

I thought about dying that night. I didn't think about how to kill myself, but I thought about what it might be like to die. This was my first experience facing my suffering honestly. It was the first time that I looked at myself clearly and acknowledged that I wasn't living a life that I thought was worth being alive for. I was convinced that a hopeless life wasn't worth living at all.

Before I could think about any ways to move forward on my deathly impulses, my rational and protective measures took over and I became overwhelmed with fear. My emotions and thoughts were so overpowering that I scared myself.

At 11:30 pm I called my mom and then my dad. It was the middle of the night on the east coast and neither of them picked up. I called my grandma, who I knew stayed up late. She picked up and I let everything gush out of me. As I talked, I calmed down. I noticed that my body had been shaking and it stopped. She listened attentively and lovingly.

I don't think I would have actively harmed myself that night. I didn't want to die; I just also didn't want to live the life I had.

I was forced to reevaluate how and why I was living my life. I instinctively knew that I couldn't live life trying to be anyone but myself anymore. (But like before, it was only the beginning.) That experience scared me enough to wake up, just a little. I went low enough into myself to see my hidden pain. I didn't know **what** to do, only that I had to **do** something different.

After that night I got caught back up in the whirlwind of my life until I had a few minutes to take a break during finals week. It was Thursday afternoon and I was in my hammock under a magnolia tree reading a book. There were no benches under the tree (yet), so I hammocked in peace.

As I turned the last page of the book about adventure, quests, and risk taking, I started to cry[1]. I was hidden in the green folds of my hammock and felt isolated enough to let real tears flow. My sadness gushed out of me in waves of unfulfillment and disappointment with my life. As my emotions poured out, I was left with a certain truth: I needed to quit my job as an RA, withdraw from school, and go on a quest. It was as if all my doubt had evaporated with my tears and only my heart's desire was left. I knew what I needed to do and it didn't matter what anyone else thought about it.

Straight from my hammock, I walked to my boss's office and had a quick conversation to let her know I was leaving. The conversation went well, given all the rules I had broken. When I quit, I felt some guilt because I was letting down my team, but it was insignificant compared to the relief I felt from finally acting on my authentic desires. Plus, I knew that I wasn't the right person for that job and that they would find someone who didn't drink and hookup with residents. There were better candidates, and I was free from my cage.

From her office, I skipped, like a four-year-old on his way to get a fudgsicle, to the registrar's office. I informed the counselor that I would be taking a quarter off from college. The process was surprisingly easy. I always imagined taking time off from school would be a giant task. I imagined that people would judge me. I imagined that it was impossible. These were all stories I told myself. In less than an hour, I had completely changed my life.

---

[1] Book: The Happiness of Pursuit by Chris Guillbeau

In the next few days, I packed my entire room, said my goodbyes to the people I cared about, flew home, and bought a ticket to Vietnam. I was going overseas for the first time.

———⟫———

You might be wondering where my parents were in all this. How could they let me withdraw from school and fly around the world, not to mention drink too much and break all the rules? I know that as a college student reading this book or as a parent of a college student, I would be wondering the same things. One is easy: I didn't tell my parents about my escapades. The other is a little more complicated.

At first, my parents were not keen on my decision to take time off from school nor were they happy that I would be spending my entire life savings to fly solo to Southeast Asia. They had a lot of questions about how it would work logistically, how I would graduate on time, and where I would go.

Beyond all these questions though, was a deeper issue. They were letting fear for me dictate their parenting. I remember directly asking my mom to "please never parent me from a place of fear again." Deciding to go to Asia on my own was my first truly independent decision where I chose authenticity and Truth over fear. I wasn't going to let anyone stop me.

My parents weren't stoked about my decision initially, but it was mine to make. I told them why I was going, assured them that I was ahead of schedule in school, and explained how I would stay safe. Eventually, they came around and supported me because they were being good parents who wanted the best for their kid. Beyond that, I somehow convinced them to trust me to make my own decisions. This was new and I loved it. Receiving my parents' trust was a powerful and new blessing.

In college, my peers often said to me: "I have to major in XYZ because my parents are paying for my degree and if I don't major in XYZ, they won't support me." There are usually two things going on here:

1. The student is doing XYZ degree because figuring out what they actually want from their lives is scarier than doing XYZ degree.

2. The parents are too afraid to let their child make their own choices and live authentically because they themselves never did.

Whenever I heard people say that, I was so disappointed with their parents. People should study what lights them up. By hindering your child's ability to find their own path and discern their own dreams, you're stopping them from finding true joy in life. If you're a parent reading this, learn to let go of the fears you have about your children and try to trust that they'll find their own way in life. Love them always and support them when you have the capacity to, but never control them, because it won't end well, ever.

By deciding to go to Asia, I took complete ownership of my life. I followed my heart and intuition. Despite everyone telling me that I was wrong, I knew I was right to take time off from school and to quest in search of meaning. I finally had a reason to live, and it made me come alive. My reason wasn't glamorous or concrete. It was to find a better reason. I woke up to my lack of direction and I sought a compass. Thus began my adventure to escape spiritual depression in earnest.

An Intermission

QUESTIONS

You must always begin your healing journey with
awareness. Awareness is the seed by which your sapling
will grow. It is the darkness moving to light. To seek
awareness is frightening and demands courage.

Ask yourself these questions:
Why am I alive?
Do I believe I am here for a reason?
Am I conscious of how my actions affect those around me?
Am I avoiding any feelings?
How am I? How am I, really?
What am I longing for?
Do I have dreams?
Am I going after my dreams?

See what comes up for you as you journey within yourself.
When you answer these questions don't turn away from
the feelings that come with those answers. If you cannot
answer one of the questions, notice that, too. There are

no wrong answers or lack thereof because all questions
of our inner selves lead to great awareness and from
awareness we may find Truth and self-love.

Part 2 is my journey into the fog of spiritual depression,
into myself, and into my pain.

PART 2
INTO THE FOG

ACCEPTANCE

"

Some students had trouble finding the name of the wind.
There were too few edges here, too little risk. So they would
go off into the wild, uneducated lands. They would seek their
fortunes, have adventures, hunt for secrets and treasure...
But they were really looking for the name of the wind.

"

— PATRICK ROTHFUSS

-5-

THE FIRST ADVENTURE

*"The purpose of life is to live it, to taste experience
to the utmost, to reach out eagerly and without
fear for newer and richer experience."*
– ELEANOR ROOSEVELT

Before flying to Asia I went back to California with a ticket I had already purchased. My flight to Asia was for the end of January and I had a few weeks with no obligations before leaving. For those few weeks, I convinced one of my best friends, Raven, to fly to CA and drive around the Southwest. I picked him up at the airport and we drove toward the coast. When we got onto Highway 1, I felt a gigantic weight fall from my shoulders. I rolled the windows down and whooped and hollered. That night, I wrote:

"Today I felt happier than I have in a long time driving down Highway 1. It's an amazing feeling to know that my actions line up with the direction of my heart. The feeling of my actions representing what was inside me was the best one in the world."

Raven and I saw glorious sights, from sunset on the ridge of Big Sur to sunrise over the Grand Canyon. We filled our days with driving, singing, talking, silence, and adventure. It was the most fun and freeing thing I had ever done.

Beyond freeing, one conversation with Raven subtly set me on a path that would unfold in front of me for years to come. At the time, I was always busy doing something. I was always busy. Raven, on the other hand, was not. I held it against him. I thought that his slow-moving life was a sign that he was incapable of doing the work necessary to live a full life. On our road trip, as we drove around a mesa in Southern Utah, I asked him why he didn't do more with his life (a stupid question to ask someone you love, but I was young and ignorant.)

Raven turned and said something along the lines of, "You don't always have to be growing, sometimes stopping is the best choice you can make." At the time, I thought this was ridiculous. How could you be moving forward unless you're growing? But, over the next few years, I would find an appreciation for slowing down that changed everything. But I'm getting ahead of myself.

Our trip ended at my cousin's house near Santa Clara. It wasn't expensive nor long, but it unlocked me and allowed me to let go of my resistance to possibility. Before I went, there was always friction for me against doing what I genuinely wanted. Once I went on this short trip, the friction started its very slow melting process. Over the next three years, it would continue to melt.

This first melting moment was pivotal because it showed me that I could live my life authentically. Until my road trip, I didn't believe that I could travel at all. This theme has continued throughout my life: Until I do something that I deeply desire, I don't believe that it's possible, but each time I try, I end up doing it. Years later, I still surprise myself when I accomplish something that I always thought was impossible. Where before I had doubt, I still have doubt. It is only natural. But now there is faith, too, that I will find my way.

Raven and I arrived back in the Bay Area. He flew home to Massachusetts while I stayed at my cousin's. I began to frantically pack all my clothes, camera gear, and other necessities into my backpacking backpack, which I stuffed inside my suitcase. I wasn't bringing much. A few changes of clothes, my camera, laptop, a journal, passport, wallet, phone, accessories, and toiletries. It was wild how little I needed to travel around the world for 6 weeks. (Hot tip: Unlock your phone for new sim cards before traveling to a different country!)

Departure day arrived and my cousin, Sue, drove me to the airport. She dropped me off and I waited in line at the China Southern Airline booth. I felt nervous. I double checked all my documents. I had my passport. I had my wallet. I had my visa paperwork. I had my ticket. I was good.

At the booth, I smiled at the Chinese man on the other side. I gave him all my paperwork, which he scanned.

When he got to the visa, he asked "Do you have the other one?" I was confused and immediately worried. I didn't know what "other one" he was talking about. After going back and forth for a few minutes, it turned out I printed the application for the visa and not the visa itself. It was a rookie mistake.

I called Sue, who was on her way to work, "Sue, I messed up my visa," I confessed. "Can you come get me?"

She couldn't come get me and recommended I take the train back to SCU for the day. Thus, my unpredictable, solo adventure began with a train back to familiar instead of a flight to the unknown. This set the stage for the rest of my travels: Cheerfully making mistakes, learning at every possible turn, and finding humility from life's teachings.

People often mistake traveling for a fun and easy thing. It's not. Traveling—especially solo—is like being a fish smack dab in the middle of an island. You flounder until someone is nice enough to put you back in the sea or until, miraculously, you flop back in. I pushed back my flight and rushed my visa application and watched my savings fall. But I was committed.

I took the train back to Santa Clara and was grateful for the pause before the storm. Raven's lesson resonated with me. Maybe what I needed was rest after all. Sometimes, the outcome of mistakes is what's best. Life goes on and it's up to us to make the most of it. This was an important lesson for me because it took pressure off my decision making for the trip and my life. I allowed myself to fail, knowing that my "failure" might be better than a planned "success."

After a harrowing journey through an overnight Chinese layover, my first destination in Asia was Ho Chi Minh City. It was a city like all others, busy with people doing all manners of things in all manners of places. There were tall buildings and squat buildings, dirty areas and clean ones. And yet it was different, too. There were coconut salespeople and hole-in-the-wall barber shops. Motorbikes were everywhere, always, teaming like schools of fish through water. And it smelled different, like hot dirt, burning trash, and exhaust.

I began my trip in Ho Chi Minh City because I had a family friend who lived there as an English teacher. One day, we went to meet a student's family for lunch in the country. As I rode behind my friend on his motorbike through villages, over rivers, and around tropical trees, I started to see Vietnam in a different light. It was beautiful and diverse, hosting bustling cities filled with commerce and endless nature, too.

We arrived and I saw a house made entirely of concrete. Inside, I noticed that there was no mattress on the bed frame and no doors on the door frames. There were no paintings or photographs on the walls.

For the first time, I viscerally felt my privilege as an American. My family never had much money compared to those around us; I got free lunches at school and my mom used WIC checks for my sisters. Until this point, I assumed I was poor. Not until I got to Vietnam did I realize how lucky I was to have a bed to sleep on and food on the table. This Vietnamese family showed me what's important in life: Gratitude and generosity.

They gave us fresh fruits from their trees and fish from their pond. We took turns whacking small bunches of water coconuts on the ground to break them and scoop out the meat (imagine a bunch of bananas or grapes but small diamond-shaped coconuts instead). Each time, I whacked the coconut bunches on the earth, they doubled over in fits of laughter. It was infectious and eventually we all brimmed with contagious glee.

They made us a home cooked meal of soup, fried rice, whole shrimps, and other things I'd never seen before. They brought us fishing in their backyard and introduced us to their extended family. I couldn't speak to them at all in words but began to understand that without words I could connect to them in deeper, more human ways. Just smiling and making eye contact was enough to show I cared about them as fellow humans. It was more than enough of a connection.

These people, with so few possessions, were filled with joy because they could share what they had. That was enough for them. Their laughs and smiles filled me with happiness and their generosity inspired me.

One night, a few days later, I was playing soccer with some locals and foreigners. I was struck by one young kind and gracious Vietnamese man on my team. He studied Environmental Science in University and clearly had a good heart and smart mind.

During a water break, I said: "If you ever want to visit the US, I'd be happy to host you!" I thought I was offering something generous.

He looked down and then said, "It's impossible for me, because I would need to save 5 years of my salary just to get the visa." I was stunned and felt guilty.

Being in Ho Chi Minh made me understand my privilege and want to use it to serve others. (File this away because it will come back later.)

———— ⟫⟫⟫ ————

I always imagined myself in Bali. When I cried in my hammock it's because I wanted so badly to be traveling in Bali. So, after Vietnam, I went. The freedom that comes from solo travel is unparalleled; at any moment you can decide to fly or drive or walk anywhere else in the world given the financial means. It's exhilarating.

Flying into Bali was surreal. I watched a volcano tower above the jungle from my plane window and realized that I was checking off an authentic dream for the first time ever. I got out of the airport to find my driver waiting for me (I paid for an overpriced tour; lesson learned) and took off toward the beach. He weaved through crowded and noisy streets full of cars, vans, busses, motorbikes, and trinket hawkers.

After checking into my hostel, I went straight to the beach. I rented a surfboard and somehow made it past the break. I struggled through the towering waves and got to the calmer waters. Even in the stillness, I kept falling over. I was surrounded by experts and felt foolish and yet, for all the struggling and lack of wave catching, I was exactly where I wanted to be: Sitting in the warm ocean, under the tropical sun, on a surfboard in Bali. It was a dream come true.

In Bali, I spent each day at the beach or wandering in sun-kissed rice fields nights, I spent at a beach club called Old Man's. At Old Mans, I fell deeply in love with a woman who was leaving Bali in two days; the fickle nature of traveling the world is beautiful and painful, tantalizing and ethereal. I felt the unmistakable feeling of falling in love but never was able to make anything of it.

A few days later, I became suddenly exhausted and soon after violently ill. It was Bali Belly, the infamous stomach bug. I was sick for a few miserable days, yet I wouldn't give those days up for anything. Despite the pain, I was exactly where I wanted to be.

I didn't completely recover from Bali Belly before leaving for Hanoi. Getting from the island off the coast, where I had been holed up, to the Denpasar airport took about 4 hours. I took a boat and then a bus and was swapped out of the bus and into a new van with a mystery driver who didn't speak English. I made it to the airport and then flew to Kuala Lumpur in Malaysia, had a 10-hour, overnight layover, which I spent on a metal bench and in the bathroom. Finally, I landed in Hanoi and took an Uber to my hostel where I collapsed into my bed and napped. When I woke up, I was finally refreshed.

Even through the struggles of Bali Belly on a plane, bus, boat, van, and plane again, I was grateful to be traveling. On the plane, flying into Hanoi, I looked out the window and at the clouds and started to cry. I was overcome with gratitude and happiness. I felt so lucky to be traveling, despite it all. I was where I wanted to be.

I traveled in 5 vehicles over 16 hours while violently ill, but I was doing exactly what I felt called to do, so I was grateful. When we step onto our authentic paths, hard things become filled with gratitude. When living authentically, pain comes and is welcome, never to be transformed into suffering. I learned this lesson for the first time in Asia, but it took me years to really integrate it into my life. I still need to remind myself today that my failure and pain in life is in service of growth, learning, and becoming me. It was a valuable lesson but didn't apply cleanly to my life back home.

Coming back from Asia, I needed to learn how to apply lessons made while "away" to my "normal" life. This is a lot like coaching. When clients come to me for our weekly calls, they open up about their insecurities and dreams. We work together to figure out who they want to be and how they're going to do it. But our coaching calls aren't their "normal" life, only a commentary on it. Asia gave me the opportunity to see myself like I give clients in coaching. I saw what my life could be, but still needed to bring that vision back. Most of the work isn't in the coaching call, but in the integration of that call with one's life. My experience in Asia was the same.

Only in retrospect can I see how much my time in Asia affected the trajectory of my life. Because I had the courage to take a leap on my dreams, I learned that I could do it again. I fell in love and lost it, learned the secrets of gratitude and generosity, recognized my privilege and a desire to do something with it, and most importantly, learned to trust the mysterious nature of life.

Over and over while I was traveling, I had to put my safety into the hands of strangers who didn't speak any English. All I had was a gut check and faith that if I was meant to live, I would. I have never lost this unconditional trust of those around me, for better or worse. I think better, but I have no proof.

When I got home, my stepdad, Jon, asked "Did you find the answers you were looking for?"

"No, but I had fun!" I said dejectedly, feeling like a failure for not finding some bigger truth.

Then he said something that I'll never forget: "You had fun! Maybe that is the answer."

The simple takeaway from my trip to Asia was that my life could be an opportunity to paint whatever kind of picture I wanted and enjoy the process of painting.

Whenever someone asks me if they should travel, I always say: "Yes! No matter what, find a way." Traveling is enlightening. Travel puts challenges in front of us and forces us to be creative. When people ask if they should hire a coach, I say the same thing. They both show us who we are.

But, travel, like coaching, requires integration. I still needed to bring my lessons back. I had no idea how hard this would be or how long it would take.

-6-

THE SPRING OF MELANCHOLY

*"I don't know what's worse: to not know what
you are and be happy, or to become what you've
always wanted to be, and feel alone."*
– DANIEL KEYES

My trip to Asia was a wonderful experience and opened my eyes to new possibilities, but ultimately it didn't provide me with the answers I was looking for. This book isn't about my travels, but the deeper reasons for wanting to travel in the first place: "Why am I alive?"

I include my trip to Asia in the book because it was the beginning. Our healing journeys are non-linear, arduous, and circuitous. Asia showed me the possibility and joy that can lie beyond our fears, but my story isn't all breakthroughs and joy.

When I got back from Asia, I dove straight back into school. Despite the fun and adventure, despite the new friends and memories, I still battled the same inner demons I had before I left. I was still trying to figure out why I was alive and for what reasons I kept on living. I was still haunted by a lack of direction and purpose in my life.

The spring after Asia was one of the numbest periods of my entire life. My memories from the spring are hazy except for a constant and incessant feeling of lack, as if I was forgetting something important.

In Asia, I felt full. After returning, I was empty again. It was confusing and, in my confusion, I turned to writing, which ranged from brokenhearted to inspirational. I was seeking answers to the dissonance in my heart through the dissonance of my words.

I was only back in SCU for one quarter before leaving to study abroad in New Zealand. I let myself drift into a liminal purgatory, distancing my awareness from my daily life. I was waiting for my "normal" life to be over so that I could travel again. I went through the motions in classes and friendships, my energy drained into keeping me alive. Before Asia, I was slowly dying with no hope for a better life. Now, I had hope, but it was only in the future. That made my present reality even worse than before.

Living inauthentically drained my energy to constantly fill the void inside. That spring, I was devoid of motivation, back under the fog of my depression and conformity. It felt like I was dragging myself through life. I was depressed, and for the first time in my adult life, aware of other options. In Asia, I had been joyful and enthusiastic; I gained an inner spark. Back at school, the contrast between my flicker of Truth and the fog of suffering tore me apart. As I was torn apart, poetry flowed out of me.

It was like my heart was breaking open. Words leaked from my fingers onto pages like blood, representing my contrasting Truth and Suffering. Here is a poem from that spring:

Inexplicable Throbbing

Inexplicably throbbing from the pain in my heart
The weight of the world seems to tear me apart.
I can't find one sense in my mind
To create a vision of things that I'll leave behind.
I know I'm not perfect. I know I have flaws
But the wounds are not so simple, to be covered with gauze.
The wounds are deep down, where it's so hard to get,
It takes real commitment to even begin to forget,
Not to mention forgive, the causes of heart wounds.
"It will be easy," my past self presumes.
Boy was I wrong, I laugh to the world,
My life has been heaved and hurled.
I heard once that gratitude is the path to move past these
Inexplicable pains that weigh down my chassis.
I look back at my life and think of the love,
The hatred, the fear, and the maybe-God up above.
Who knows what will heal me but time and good faith
That the life I am living is not simply a wraith
Of the dreams that I have and goals that I've set.

Hopefully one day, these things will be met.
Until that day, onward, I'll fight through the fear
Of drowning in sorrow every day here.
It's but a choice, I've been told,
To get a grip and be bold,
But when I face it in life,
It feels more like strife,
It's more realistic and harder to fight.
Who even knows what's wrong and what's right?
With my time on this Earth, I hope I can live,
With the gusto to dream and the light to forgive.

My heart tore open and I saw my pain verbalized. Those months were a springboard for my inner reflection. I had no choice but to face my pain and unresolved trauma head on just to survive each day. Poetry introduced me to my heart and to the pain I was holding in a way I could put into words. When I was sad, I let my heart write poems. I leaned on poetry to show me my pain. I learned about myself and acknowledged my pain and suffering through the flow of words. I learned how to write from my heart, and it showed me what I needed to see.

When I went to New Zealand in June, my poetry, pain, and internal revolution only intensified. I was starting to break out of my inner cage and do the hard work of healing. I just didn't know it yet.

-7-

POETRY POURS FORTH

"All that is gold does not glitter,
Not all those who wander are lost;
The old that is strong does not wither,
Deep roots are not reached by the frost.
From the ashes a fire shall be woken,
A light from the shadows shall spring;
Renewed shall be blade that was broken,
The crownless again shall be king."
— JRR TOLKIEN

My time in Middle Earth exactly wasn't what I was expecting. After traveling in Asia, I thought that New Zealand would be another joyful adventure filled with lessons. I was half right. There were a lot of lessons. The joy: Harder to come by.

When I got there, it was late June. Summer, right?! Wrong: the southern hemisphere was in the prime of winter. I went from sunny, 85° California to rainy, 37° New Zealand. I brought all my melancholy, and the weather didn't help. I still felt empty inside and now I contended with seasonal depression and a totally new culture, too.

For the first two months in New Zealand, I was incredibly depressed; I drank more than ever, and I let my sexual self go wild. All my vices came out to play and played hard. Even more than in my sophomore year, I was escaping my inner traumas. In my melancholy spring, pain started to flow out of me in waves of meaninglessness. In New Zealand, it got even more intense, so I tried to shut it down. I skipped classes and stayed in bed until after noon. I felt hopeless and couldn't think straight or motivate myself.

On July 25th, about a month after getting to New Zealand, I wrote the following: "Every day I feel my brain fog up, like a windshield on a rainy night. It's weird. My mind is numb and less sharp. I hope there's nothing seriously wrong with me." This was my main symptom—a fog in my head preventing me from experiencing the world with any clarity or intentionality. I was a wisp of myself, carried on the wind from place to place. I think I had been a wisp for years, I just had never noticed before. I didn't have the awareness yet.

This went on for weeks. I don't remember much except for binging on cheap alcohol, TV, and sleep—oh, and the incessant rain. I spent most of my time in bed or out drinking. I didn't care about my classes at all. I couldn't see that my suffering, the fog, was caused by avoiding my pain.

For weeks, I beat myself up without awareness. Then about two months in, I realized that I wasn't alive. Sure, my body was waking up and going through the motions. I could have conversations and I could make myself eggs for breakfast. But was I really *living my life*? No.

I was extremely socially anxious in New Zealand. I felt unworthy and didn't know why. I felt uncomfortable and scared talking to everyone. I was scared to say my true thoughts. I feared life because I wasn't living it for the right reasons or any reasons at all, really. The world around me was a constant reminder that I wasn't who I wanted to be, that there was another version of me out there. Every interaction and every person made me remember that I didn't know why I was alive. When I saw happy people, I wondered how they smiled. When I saw depressed and sad people or people drinking too much at parties, I wondered if they, like me, were lost in the world and didn't know why they were alive.

At the time, I couldn't explain my depression and anxiety. It was a dark haze of hopelessness and lack of motivation. I was too ashamed to talk to anyone about my darkness. I didn't feel like I could trust anyone with the weight I carried around, and thus I felt desperately alone.

I was in a fog, thicker than I had ever experienced. I wasn't present in the world. I was lost, like a sleepwalking automaton. It was a return to my high school self, except my pain was much closer to surfacing. Instead of pure numbness, it was painful and hazy, challenging and meaningless—the worst of both worlds.

Throughout this chapter are poems from my time in New Zealand to show you what I was going through firsthand.

The Fog in My Head

There is an eerie mist,
That lies just out of reach
The fog is out beyond the beach
And it feels like I have no vessel,
I have no form of transportation
And feel only desperation.

I need a ship to sail.

To be real, my ship can be built,
From the pieces just beyond my guilt.
I'm stopped short of first,
Striving not to be the worst.
The painful monotonous drifting
Without the fog ever lifting.
It's not so complicated
And it's not to be hated,
That the key to the ship,
Lies in the rise from the dip,
Stemming from our power
To with our energy devour,
The daunting mist lying in wait,
That we so seem to hate.

An act of commitment,
To bringing forth my best,
A feeling of not belonging
To the lazy world of rest.
I will captain my own galley,
I will steer my own tomorrow
Against the fog I must rally,
To stop is to succumb to the sorrow.

Fight the exhibitions
Of meaningless missions
And bring to life your wish
Like casting for the fish
Lying out of sight
Out into the night.
By putting out your hook,
You're opening the book
That in it will be scribed,
The life that you've been bribed
To leave in your heart and your head,
To leave until you're dead.
Take up arms against the tyranny
And live your own verity.

Beat back the fog,
With everything you've got,
For if you don't, in the bog,
You'll be left to rot.

The only "memories" I have of this time are poems. Each poem expresses the True self that I was searching for and the fog surrounding it. As I go back to read my poetry, I see a boy becoming a man. I see a traumatized, sleeping version of myself shedding his skin and diving inside himself. Each poem expresses the darkness I felt and yet shows signs of hope, of introspection, and of changing tides. I was revolting against the pressures that I had let dictate my life until that moment. I was coming alive, but it was incredibly painful because I had to shed my old life. The process of shedding made me feel gross, vulnerable and exhausted. And yet, I still wrote poem after poem expressing my transformation, my shame, and my anger.

Grave Error

I want to break things,
I want to hurl myself into the abyss,
I need to see how broken I can get,
So I know that I'm not a dick
Who has been throwing his seconds away.

Before New Zealand, my subconscious mind was aware that I had been wasting my life away. Now, my conscious mind knew it. Poetry bridged the two parts of my mind.

The process of realizing that I had wasted years of my life broke me. Luckily, it was a break down and a breakthrough. As I broke, the light came in. As my shell shattered, I finally saw my inner child. I saw his trauma and his dreams. I saw his grief and let it fill me.

Through the Cracks

Slipping through the cracks,
Glimmers of what could be.
Walled off from the beauty,
The beauty of being free.

Curled in a ball, practiced for years,
Unable to escape the paralyzing fears.
These fears for so long thought to be
Ways to be free, to be me.
To escape the painful nature of love,
And escape to a world up above,
Going with the flow,
Taking it slow... Now I know.

Those walls weren't safe,
They were a cage,
I was locked in.
Now, today, I must be a mage,
I must free myself, break out,
I must turn the page.

Each blank page is rife with chances,
Each new day full of potential dances

With destiny, with lovely ladies,
With my heart, with destination Hades.
Life is for living, I keep saying,
And yet here I am praying
That someone will come pull me out
And with my old life, make a rout.
I can't do it myself, I think,
I would need to push myself to the brink.

It's a decision, Faolan.
Do you want to be free?

After months of reflecting, I saw the choice but didn't know how to execute it. My fear of letting go of my old self was stopping me from moving forward. For three months, I saw my choice and was desperate to make it yet couldn't. I was in so much pain. In retrospect, it was the pain of coming alive and of accepting my traumas. I made the painful decision to accept pain. It was the most important three months of my life.

Eventually, my poems became less depressed and more angry, driven, and powerful. I stopped moping and got pissed off at myself, at the world, and at everything. It was a shock to my system to be so upset with myself and the way I was living. I went from numb to furious. The following poems show how my depression turned to anger, anger to resentment of self, and from resentment to courage.

Ducks in a Row

Neat little folds, each corner meticulously made just so.
Everything is organized, planned, all my ducks in a row.
Bullshit.
It just doesn't fit.
This life of mine, droning away,
It's supposed to be a time to play,
That's what I've heard from some.
Who fucking knows? Bang the drum,
It's time for a war,
Don't hit snooze, don't snore.
It's not going to be easy or even fun
But this life needs to be shot with a gun.
What a waste, shitting it down the drain,
"Oh my, every day is such a fucking pain."
Do you hear your voice?
Get a grip, you have a choice.
This will end right now.
Boom, bang, pow.
Everything will change,
I will take the measures to rearrange
This monotonous, painstakingly boring,
Life through which I'm snoring.
Why the fuck can't I find a cause?
I'm scared shitless - permanent pause.
Hit fucking play, stop quaking in your boots.
Life doesn't wait, pull up your roots,

And fucking give it your all,
Stop being small.
Fuck that. Fuck this.
There's nothing here I'm going to miss.
Climb the hill, fall down,
Just don't lie in your own piss and drown.
Fuck.
Just start.

Unnamed 3

There are people out there dying,
You understand me?
Dying. Not sleeping, not living on the edge,
They're fucking dead.
Who the fuck are you to waste your life?
You don't have a cause?
You don't know why you're doing it?
Fuck you.
Do you know how much of an opportunity you have?
Jesus fucking Christ,
Each and every day to you is a joke.
You wake up, eat like a fucking poor ass king,
Waste your time watching meaningless hypnotoad,
Sometimes do some things you've been told,
And then waste your energy pining on sex,
Pursuing acceptance, worse than sins, worse than drugs.

You grovel at the feet of people you don't even know.
You're fucking better than that.
What the fuck do you want you piece of shit?

I want to live, I want to strive,
I want to give, I want to thrive.
Specifically, I don't fucking know,
I want to put on a show,
Give it my all,
Go fucking get big and tall.
I want people to look at me and know.
Really fucking know that they can grow.
I want to inspire.
I want to acquire.
I want to ascend.
I want to bend.
I want to bend the rules,
Create new tools,
For the average Jack, the average Jill,
To learn their route up the fucking hill.
We all have our mountains,
We all have our fountains.
Climb the route,
Burst forth, don't be moot.
I will become a king.
I will wear the ring.
I will be the champion of my life,
I will beat my chest, I will walk the knife.

The edge between false and true.
Between me and you,
I know I have the answers,
Right now, I'm stuck with them - All glancers.
Too afraid to jump in,
Just catching fleeting glances of the grin
On that guy, oh that fucking guy,
Who I look up to. He shows me it's all a lie.
Everything I've known.
Everything I've been shown.
Life is for the taking,
So stop your fucking shaking.
And take it all back,
Create everything you lack.

THE BATTLE IS OVER

The battle is over, the battle is won.
I can no longer hear the beating of drums.
The light has returned and the sun once more rises,
Blessing this life so full of brightness—It galvanizes.
I've fought and I've fought for the right to free,
When all along it's been right in front of me.
I can't believe it has taken this long
To acquiesce to the words of the song.
I longed and strived for the feelings inside
To lead to serenity, to keep me alive.
It's with a sigh of relief that I step back on land
From the raging sea, on which I took my stand.

The battle is over, I've returned from the fight,
Welcoming home the blessed light.
With me I bring gifts from faraway lands,
That I leave for the people in the beach's gold sands.
Except for the one that in my heart will be kept,
Over which, for forever, I once wept.

Phew! Can you feel my anger? It was overpowering. As it boiled, like spitting water flying from a pot, it burned me. My anger woke me up with pain and made me choose myself, with all my suffering, resentment, and rage. It made me acutely see my True self and it hurt.

My time in Middle Earth was the hardest of my life. I was empty. I was afraid to be myself. Even the thought of being me, authentically, and without hesitation caused me so much anxiety I physically felt pain. Every moment was a scrape against the blackboard, a moan of the sick. I was dying, not living, and yet paradoxically coming alive.

My rage woke me up to my emptiness. I saw my emptiness and for the first time wasn't resigned to its continued existence. I wanted it gone, no matter what. I was done suffering.

So, I set aside my responsibilities, my friendships, and my society. I stopped going to class altogether, didn't see friends, or talk to anyone. Instead, I devoured books, searched my soul, experienced great moments of sadness, lost track of days and weeks, and finally found myself sitting on a bench in the botanical gardens.

An Intermission

EMOTION EVOLUTION

Often when we're resisting reality we feel emotions like anger, frustration, resentment, jealousy, and shame. These emotions are born from awareness of reality without acceptance of reality. When we accept our reality, these emotions evolve from external projections to internal transformations.

Anger often becomes sadness or grief, which evolves into processing and growth.

Frustration or annoyance can become boundaries.

Resentment can become gratitude.

Jealousy can help us learn what we want and let go of what we wish we had.

Shame can teach us how to grow.

In New Zealand my anger with myself and with the world around me transformed through poetry and pausing into an opportunity for me to learn and grow. When we slow down and breathe into our emotions, we open the door to what they can evolve into. Only by making time to accept reality and feel the deeper emotions under our surface emotions can we truly heal our innermost hurts.

When we do, things can change very quickly. Practice awareness and acceptance in order to awaken.

PART 3
THE SWITCH

AWAKENING

"

Trials never end, of course. Unhappiness and misfortune are bound to occur as long as people live, but there is a feeling now, that was not here before, and is not just on the surface of things, but penetrates all the way through: We've won it. It's going to get better now. You can sort of tell these things.

"

— ROBERT PIRSIG

-8-

KATHUNK

"I saw in the story about Moses and the burning bush, Moses doesn't take his sandals off because suddenly the ground becomes holy. The ground has been holy the whole time. The story is about Moses becoming aware of it."
– ROB BELL

I'm rather fond of benches in beautiful places, benches that feel like resting places amidst the flurry of life. This bench in the botanical gardens was one such bench. A tree, covered in small yellow flowers, hung above me. In front of me, a view of the city of Dunedin and the mountains beyond. To my left was the trail from where I had come and to my right, a small field, and on this day, a few ducks.

The past week was an unusual one. The weather warmed slightly and with it, my mood. I skipped all my classes and spent my time reading Steve Jobs by Walter Isaacson. I was fascinated by his spirituality, his obsession with perfection, and his unwavering belief in his own purpose.

At the end of the book is a quote he played at his funeral service: "Here's to the crazy ones. The misfits. The rebels. The troublemakers. The round pegs in the square holes. The ones who see things differently." As I read that, I leaned back on the bench and thought of another book that said the same thing with different words: Zen and the Art of Motorcycle Maintenance by Robert Pirsig (ZAMM). I had finished ZAMM already but was called to read the ending again. I took it out of my backpack and with Jobs' words echoing in my mind, read again. I'm not going to spoil the ending because I believe if you like my book, you should read ZAMM, too. That being said, it's a beautiful end full of love, acceptance, and relief.

As I came to the end of ZAMM, I felt a primal surge from deep inside me, energy trapped there splitting its shell and breaking free after years of confinement. The overpowering energy made me cry. They weren't tears of sadness or grief, but joy. My tears were because I witnessed, with clarity, the journey that takes us from heretic to hero.

The word heretic always stood out to me. People name those who challenge "normal," heretics. Heretics are the ones who, like Copernicus, find new revelations and bring them to the attention of the status-quo. Society doesn't take kindly to heretics, at least not at first. But eventually, heretics become the heroes, the people who are willing to be ridiculed in the eyes of the many because they deeply believe in their Truth. George Orwell said, "Being in a minority, even in a minority of one, does not make you mad. There is truth and there is untruth, and if you cling to the truth even against the whole world, you are not mad."[2]

Heretics are harbingers of change and bear the burden of carrying Truth and on that day, I became a heretic.

I finished the book, tears streaming down my face and walked into the forest behind my bench to pee. I looked up into the trees above me, seeing every vein in every leaf. Time froze and suddenly I felt something happen. It was as if a cosmic ghost plummeted from space and hit me squarely in the chest. My hands went back as I felt a physical sensation in my body. Immediately, I knew what had happened: My soul returned to me with a great KATHUNK!!!!

In that moment, after 10 years of hiding under layers of suffering, my childhood soul came back. For years, I was a shell of myself; empty. For years, I suffered in darkness and carried the weight of unhealed pain. Suddenly, the void in my heart was filled and I felt whole. The feeling was immediate. I knew it, profoundly. And with my soul, came my purpose for being alive. I couldn't understand it or articulate it, but I felt it there inside me.

With the return of my soul came meaning and love. With the return of myself, came a direction to fight in and a reason to be alive. I couldn't name my direction or the reason, but I could feel them. For the first time in 10 years, I felt the indescribable awe of being alive. It was like being brought into the light from darkness.

[2] Adjusted to be in present tense.

When I finished reading *ZAMM* for the second time, I welcomed my soul, love, and purpose back into my life. I did the work to bring my soul back and knew that I would never lose it again. There would be times of darkness to come and there would be lows, but I would face them as my whole self. I would break open and through many times more and I would experience loss, but I would do it all as my true self. I was me, whole again and awake for the first time since I was a child.

An Intermission

THE SWITCH EXPLAINED

You should know that my "KATHUNK" experience is not necessary for each person to have. We all have mystical experiences on our spiritual paths. Mine felt like this and happened at a time when I was coming through the tunnel of darkness. Your awakening moments will feel like yours, not mine, and that is as it is meant to be. Start with awareness of yourself and you will see yourself changing. Sometimes, slowly and sometimes suddenly. When it happens suddenly, notice how it feels and what has changed. That is all I did.

My story changes shape now. This is the turning point. It's the point when I finally begin my true quest into the unknown as a whole self. For the first time, I had a real reason to live.

From here on, my story is all authentic, though not easy or always aware. Just because I had my soul back, didn't mean life became a walk in the park. It was still very, very hard, but finally I lived as my full, whole, and authentic self.

Imagine that each human life is like a plant. When we are born, we are seedlings under the earth waiting for water, reaching toward sunshine. While under the earth and dirt and loam, we're in total darkness. We can feel a lack of something, of sunshine, of the wind, of other trees. We are unaware of what it is that we're missing and yet aware that we are missing something. We start to shoot buds out of our seed pod, we start to feel our way toward the sun, intuitively heading in the right direction. We pull nourishment from the very earth around us that has been blocking the light from reaching our hearts. The earth that has stopped us from being the plant that we're destined to become is now feeding us and helping us become that very plant. Then, suddenly we burst through the earth and into the daylight. We feel our first touch of sunshine. Light and energy course through us.

This is how I felt when my soul returned. As if I went from being a sprout under the earth to being a sprout above the earth, I went from being in total darkness to being in the light. Not much else changed. I was still growing upward, slowly toward the sun. I didn't suddenly become a tree; I was still a sprout. What changed was my awareness of life. I was no longer intuitively feeling my way through the darkness, now I knew light, I was aware of what I had been striving for the whole time and I reveled in my awareness. I finally felt like I was going in the right direction because I could feel the sun warming me after years under the earth.

The sun represented something beyond my comprehension. I could finally feel the warmth on my skin and the lightness in my heart, but its source was a mystery to me. I grew out of the earth and into the world above in a buildup of music, like a flourishing crescendo. I journeyed within to find my unresolved pains and I discovered the truth of my being. It was now time for me to venture back home as a whole person once more, and this time show my true self to the world. Little did I know how challenging it would be.

PART 4
THE FOG LIFTS

ALIGNMENT

"

There's no point to lessons that don't bring with them pain.
People can't gain anything without sacrificing something,
after all. But once you've successfully endured that pain,
you gain a heart that is stout enough to not be overcome by
anything. Yeah, a heart made fullmetal.

"

— FULLMETAL ALCHEMIST BROTHERHOOD

-9-

RETURNING HOME

*"The most important way to offer tribute to one's
parents is by living a life of happiness and virtue.
That is the best way to repay our debt of gratitude
and to fulfill our parent's aspirations for us."*
– THE BUDDHA
THICH NHAT HANH

In November, I returned home from New Zealand, a whole person. Going home brought resolution and new challenges.

First, I went to see my mom in Eastern Florida. One afternoon, we went for a walk through a forest of scraggly trees and Spanish moss. It was approaching sunset and as we walked on a bridge over a narrow, man-made inlet of water, I asked my mom to tell me about my life before I was born, or rather her life with my dad.

My mom told me about how she and my dad started dating and drove around the country in a white VW bus. The two of them, only 18 and 21 at the time, set off together, fresh into the relationship, for a long road trip.

They drove from Massachusetts, along the west coast, meeting friends and family and Navajo elders. They saw the Grand Canyon and Sedona and the towering redwoods of California. Somewhere along the way, accidentally, I was conceived.

I was born at home on February 28th at 12:27 pm.

For the next 8 months, my mom and dad were together and despite their love for each other, they fought and argued. Eventually, they split up, and I stayed mostly with my mom.

While my mom told me the story, I came to understand how young my parents were when I was born. For the first time, I had empathy for them and was grateful. I realized how hard it must have been for a couple kids with a baby to heal their personal traumas, make money, find their vocational paths, raise me, and enjoy living. For years, I resented my parents for yelling at each other and for causing me pain but finally was able to forgive them because I put myself in their shoes.

As a child, I played the role of the intermediary, always in the middle of their tension, their resentment for each other. My trauma and pain stemmed from that tension and the feeling of carrying the weight alone. It wasn't my weight to carry at all, though. It was theirs. I simply thought that it was mine because I was born into it. When my soul returned, I accepted my history and was able to give myself love and acceptance. Because I could be myself with all my pain, I could love my parents with theirs.

Later that winter, my dad and I drove down a back road in the Berkshires. It was the dead of winter at dusk. The weather was cold and the roads were dark. As we drove, we passed thousands of snow-covered trees, shadowed in the dark of evening. I asked my dad the same question: Would he share with me about my life from before I was alive?

My dad shared many of the same feelings of pain that my mom did. He said that it was hard to watch me grow up from afar because he loved me so much. He echoed the challenge of being a young person with a child in a strained relationship. He spoke to the challenges of deciding between moving for work and staying near me. He explained how hard it was to finish college even though he knew it meant spending less time with me. It put things in perspective.

After hearing about his journey as a father, I gained the same empathy for him that I had for my mom. I had nothing but love and gratitude for my dad because I saw his past self as someone my age. I didn't think I would have handled the situation better and was able to forgive him.

Learning to accept my trauma was a powerful step in my journey to forgive my parents. In letting my resentment for myself be replaced with love, gratitude, and empathy, I was empowered to do the same for them.

Because I had the courage to begin my own healing process, I was able to ask them healing questions. Because I was vulnerable and honest with them, they felt safe to be vulnerable and honest with me. That winter, my relationships with my parents started to heal and our bonds grew stronger.

Since then, my parents have been some of my best friends. I learned to be honest with them about what I was going through and in return, they learned how to trust me, not as they would a child or an adolescent, but as an adult.

All my clients share with me about their parental relationships. They share their resentment for the way their parents treated or treat them, or the shame of not being who their parents want them to be. They often feel afraid of being vulnerable with their parents because they might hurt their parents or feel hurt by their parents. This lack of vulnerability is what causes us to suffer as adults because our childhood trauma is being repressed and unexpressed. In order to heal our trauma, we must face it.

It's important to differentiate between what I call macro-trauma and micro-trauma. Macro-trauma comes from isolated events that shake us to our core; they're damaging, scary, and hurtful. Micro-trauma comes by way of small incidents over a long period of time. Often our society discredits the second kind, but if it makes us feel bad about ourselves or lose trust for ourselves, then it's trauma.

Often our trauma is connected to our parents. This is not to say that parents always cause trauma but that kids always gain trauma, and it almost always comes by way of the parents. Parents who traumatize their children often aren't bad people but are struggling with their own insecurities and inner battles. Because they're distracted by their own suffering, they expose their children to pain. It's not purposeful or malicious, but it is what happens.

I held onto my resentment for my parents for many years because in order to let it go, I had to heal myself. Before I could forgive them, I had to forgive myself.

The truth is that every parent does the best that they can. To expect more than that is not reality. So, as a parent, don't ever feel guilty about how you parented. If you regret something, tell your child. If you need to heal yourself, heal yourself. Own your shortcomings but do not regret them, fix them. Be open and vulnerable about your pain and the challenges of being a parent and of being a person. Relationships can only heal through Truth. Don't hold back who you are. Be compassionate by opening up about your own challenges, insecurities, and dreams. Your children, no matter their age, will thrive on authentic and vulnerable connection with you.

Children, be vulnerable with your parents and let go of your shame and resentment. In order to move forward in life with powerful authenticity and agency, you must not victimize yourself. Until you forgive your parents and own your life, you won't move forward. In fact, wherever your trauma comes from, forgive! Until you're not attached to your trauma, you won't be able to move on from it. Blame and victimization de-empower you. Learn to have empathy for the people who have caused you pain and your life will become much lighter. This doesn't mean that you must keep the sources of trauma in your life, but let go of the weight and heaviness of carrying resentment around with you. Forgive to move forward.

You may have resistance to this idea. You may think your trauma is more intense than mine, and maybe it is. But truthfully, all trauma shares the same outcome. It festers inside us and causes us to suffer until we learn to accept it and love it. Once we love our trauma, we're able to forgive the people or situations that caused it. (Sneak peek: Once we forgive it, we can move forward and stop it from happening to other people.) Especially if your trauma came from someone who loves you, let it go.

Here's what I've realized about love and relationships. If someone loves you for the right reasons, it doesn't matter what you've done, they'll keep loving you. If they don't love you for the right reasons, you don't want them in your life. It's a hard Truth. People who love you deserve the whole you with all your pain and baggage. People who don't love you fully don't deserve any of you. It is often painful, but it is also simple.

That being said, your loved ones are often deeply invested in their versions of what success means. When you share yourself with loved ones or share a way you've grown, remember that they have traumas of their own, which may prevent them from understanding you. The people who love us may not understand us, especially when we grow, but that's okay. Someone doesn't need to understand us to love us, and we don't need to be understood to be loved. This was a lesson I struggled to learn when I got home from New Zealand as a changed self.

Everyone I saw at home—my old friends, family members, and acquaintances—wanted to know how my travels had been and I wanted to tell them, but I couldn't. I didn't have the vocabulary to describe in a way that they could understand what I had experienced and how I had changed. I wanted to be understood but wasn't. Because people didn't understand me, I had to practice understanding myself. But more than understanding, I had to learn to love myself as I was, without being able to comprehend who I was. This is total self-acceptance/self-love.

In a sense, my journey so far was on two paths, which sometimes intersected: one of growth and one of understanding that growth. The key piece connecting the two was self-love. Without a container of self-love, I felt alone and misunderstood, which put my growth at risk. With the container, my loneliness transformed into solitude and my misunderstanding from others became understanding of self. Self-love began my deep inner integration of growing and knowing.

In late December, I spent a few days in my family's empty house to contemplate self-love. I sat on a maroon couch by an open fireplace watching flames dance and shadows follow them like mimics. I heard the crackling of logs catching and sparking into life and I felt the sullen silence of a heavy snowfall outside, the way only snow can sound, like less than nothing at all.

As I took in the beauty of the winter day and settled into the present moment, I was able to see myself as someone different. Slowing down in peace and quiet let me have a true awareness of myself, as if I was seeing myself from outside my body.

I drifted outside my conscious, subjective awareness and looked at the person sitting on the couch below. I was overcome with pride and love for this young man. I acknowledged the suffering he had shouldered, the addictions he had battled, the pain he had felt, and the mistakes he had made. I saw his shadow side, and I also saw his gifts and his love, his joy and his spiritual essence. I didn't understand everything yet, but I saw it.

I saw myself fully and was able to have empathy for the pain that I had hidden away and the suffering it had caused. I was able to respect myself for owning my pain, learning to find awareness, and venturing into the fog of suffering. I was able to love myself because I had grown into someone who was finding meaning in his days on Earth, despite not having a full understanding of that self or that meaning.

I saw myself for who I was, without illusions. I saw the work that I had done and was proud. Yet, I also knew that my work was just beginning. It was a daunting, wonderful, enlightening moment of clarity where I saw myself as I was and loved myself in all my shortcomings. It was from this place that I wrote myself a letter on New Year's Eve.

Dear Faolan,

It's December 31, 2018. I'm sitting at my desk at my Grandparents' house. It's 1:34 in the morning and I'm feeling like I need to write a letter to myself. I've been running around the house, brainstorming, writing, thinking, repeating for the last hour and everything I've put on paper is shit. Finally, I realized that what I'm trying to do is tell myself something. As much as my writing speaks to people sometimes, it's always for me; it's to help me uncover what the truth of myself is and what the truth of life is. Writing draws out from me the things that I can't put together in my head. So, here is a letter to me, addressed to you.

Faolan, it's been twenty years, and almost twenty-one, that you have been alive. You have been waking up in the morning and going to bed at night for 7,611 days now. I had to look up how many days and I smiled to myself because that's not too many. Imagine the significance of today, dude! I'm getting ahead of myself though. The point is: I don't think that you have engaged fully. I think you're hiding because you're afraid of what you can do. You're afraid of what lies around the corner. It's something you've known about for a while. Don't get me wrong, you've made big strides so far. You have built up your armor, you've found your weapons, your tools, and your people. It's amazing how far you have come, and I love you so much for it. Really, the sheer magnitude of transformation is amazing.

Remember when you wrote some rap songs when you were 18? Those were awful, weren't they? Remember when you used to play video games for hours every day? That was a drag, wasn't it? Remember a few months ago when every day your head was full of fog and your heart was a lumpy, aching mess? Look at yourself in the mirror today! You love what you see! Sure, maybe you could turn your flab into abs or your zits into perfection, but really what's the most important part? It's not what you see in the mirror but who. And let me tell you, who you are is flourishing!

Let me remind you of some of the things you have said over the last few weeks. "This is the happiest I've felt since I could understand what happiness feels like." "I am more excited about life than I ever have been." You have grown emotionally, intellectually, physically, and spiritually so much. It's fascinating to see the changes that have followed your dedication to growth. Your search is finding gold, my friend, finally.

I am writing to you for two main reasons. One, I want to let you know how much I truly love you because of who you are inside and out. Two, I want to give you a kick in the rump to get your butt out there and to start living today!

You always tell people that you'll start saving money when you have a "real" income or that you're looking forward to "real" life. Let me tell you something that I just learned in this amazing film called Van Wilder (a tribute to my later self who will laugh at this being "the amazing film"): Real life doesn't exist tomorrow or yesterday. Real life is right now, and only right now. Are you fulfilled with what you're doing right now?

Do you love who you spend time with and what you spend your time on? Are your todays directed at intentional tomorrows? You only get so much time and yet you have such a surplus of days to spend following your dreams.

Let me remind you what those are:

1. *To be a musician and create an album*
2. *To be a best-selling author*
3. *To graduate college and show yourself that you can*
4. *To live all over the world*
5. *To create your own income streams and never sit at a desk in a tall building*
6. *To grow to your maximum potential*
7. *To be excellent by choice, every day*

Why wait? Tomorrow is a new year and with it comes a new day. Engage Fao, embrace who you are, and enjoy life because you only get one. Don't be afraid to live fully and be a goofball, don't hold back, follow your insecurities and see where they lead you, do what you love and try what you think you hate. Follow your gut. You know the truth inside yourself, so just let your heart guide you and you'll be fine, more than fine, even, excellent. Let this year be the best year of your life. There's nothing stopping you but you.

I LOVE YOU SO MUCH AND SO DO MANY OTHER PEOPLE. Don't forget this.
Much love,
Faolan Sugarman-Lash, 1st person

This letter was a premonition, a harbinger of what was to come. Little did I know, but the letter would set the stage for the next two years of my life. That letter was the slow-moving current beneath the sometimes-frozen surface of the river of my life. I wasn't always aware that I was moving in the direction I named in my letter, but I always was. Sometimes, all I was aware of was the ice covering the surface of my soul, and like all ice, it was cold and hard, but thawed eventually.

-10-

BACK TO THE DOLDRUMS

"There is the solitude of suffering, when you
go through darkness that is lonely, intense,
and terrible. Words become powerless to
express your pain; what others hear from
your words is so distant and different from
what you are actually suffering."
– JOHN O'DONOHUE

My return to Santa Clara in January of 2019 was the most painful time of my life. You might be surprised by this, considering that I had just come awake, resolved some of my trauma and resentment towards my parents, and started to love myself. But, often, it is when we grow and return to old environments that we struggle most. So it was for me.

Remember the seed that broke through the earth to feel sunlight and find awareness for the first time? Imagine that the seedling was scooped out of the Earth and flown thousands of miles away to be planted in different soil around different trees. It would be rather shocking and sudden for the seedling. That was what it was like for me to return to Santa Clara after my awakening. I didn't know how to interact with people and people didn't know who I was anymore, but they thought they did.

In my friendships, I had to relearn how to interact with people. In many ways the experience of not being understood or accepted for who I had become turned me off to life more than being asleep in the first place. Before my Kathunk, I had been lost, I hadn't felt like a whole person. After my Kathunk I found myself again, and felt whole, but I still had to live the life of the person I had been before.

This is an important concept to understand. When we change and grow into someone new—especially when we do it outside what one of my clients calls "regularly scheduled programming"—we must change our external environment to suit the new versions of who we are. Because I had grown and changed so much in New Zealand, the life I returned to in Santa Clara was clearly no longer the life I wanted. But old habits die hard.

Clients often come to me asking for help because they've noticed that they're self-sabotaging their dreams. They tell me that their dream is to be a singer but that they don't sing, or they share with me their aspiration to be an influencer but they don't post on social media. Why do people get in their own way? This is an important question and there are two answers.

1. People are unaware of life and of their true selves. This is where I was before my Kathunk. This manifests as a fear of doing inner work. i.e. Changing yourself.

2. People are alive and full of authenticity but don't know how to direct their newfound energy. This is how I was after my Kathunk. This manifests as a fear/resistance to doing outer work. i.e. Changing your environment.

I was firmly in the second category. I had come back into myself and felt alive and motivated to live my life well, but didn't know how. So, I started where we all start when we bring awareness to our lives for the first time: How life was before that awareness existed. I began the process of changing my outside world by seeing how my newly aware, authentic self responded to my environment. What other options did I have? I needed to start somewhere and where I already was, was the best (and only) option.

When I went back into my life, it was like dealing with the repercussions of a blind man arranging my furniture. Before my Kathunk I was blind to what was working and not working and so I made a mess of things. After my Kathunk I had to live in that mess and deal with the repercussions from my past self. This was a painful experience full of spiritual stubbed toes and choice curse words.

I threw myself viciously back into school, hoping that I would like it more than before. One of the decisions that my blind/sleeping self had made was to be a business management major. He did an *okay* job picking a major. But, because "past me" chose to graduate through the business school, I now had to take all the required business classes, and boy did those classes rankle awake me.

One such class was named OMIS 34, otherwise known as *Operations and Management Information Systems #34 - Science, Information Technology, Business, and Society.* (If you blacked out while you read the title, don't worry, that's the point of including it.)

It's possible that the class could have been cool, but it wasn't. It was a class about the history of technology, siloed information systems, and database management. These things could be interesting if taught using a hands-on method, but this class taught them in the abstract. Imagine learning about what databases are and how they're used and what their different parts are called without ever actually seeing a real database. This class was torture for me.

My other classes followed similar lines to this one. I had meaningless group projects and too many meetings. I had tests that made me prove my knowledge of abstract ideas that didn't matter to me in the slightest. I was going through the motions of my past life and each second was agony.

My job was another low point. I worked as an intern for a startup focusing on cryptocurrency tax laws. For someone like myself who recently became fascinated by spirituality and personal flourishing, tax law was as far as possible away from what lit my spark.

On top of the company's industry being completely foreign to my interest, I believed that it was destined to fail. In my first week on the job, I did a competitor analysis, looking for other companies doing similar things. I found countless other companies that were all much more successful, some with funding already. My heart was not in the work at all.

One day, I sat in my room writing a blog post about cryptocurrency tax laws. I stared at my computer screen for minutes on end without writing a word. My brain felt like a watermelon in flight, full of water and powerfully forced toward the earth by gravity, ready to explode into a thousand bits of mushy, red, goo. I couldn't muster the willpower to think about the topic at all, let alone write about it. I couldn't even motivate myself with the chance to earn some money because it was an unpaid internship that was required to graduate. It felt like slowly drowning myself in molasses. I was sinking deeper into the old life that I knew was wrong for me, but, at the time, didn't believe that I could do anything about it.

I'm careful with my language here. It's not that I couldn't change anything but that I believed I couldn't. I had the power to change my situation (and later would), but I didn't. In reality, we almost always have the power to change our situations but often don't because we are attached to the path that we've been on and to change our situations would be to change our path and venture into the unknown, away from what is comfortable. To venture into the unknown is scary and, inevitably, the only path available to continue living authentically and escape self-perpetuated suffering.

At the time, I had no idea that I could change my everyday life, I was simply bogged down by my ex-self's choices. I felt stuck writing meaningless blogs for a meaningless company and doing meaningless projects for meaningless classes. Needless to say, my life didn't feel very meaningful.

For years, my old self conformed to society's expectations of him. After my Kathunk, I didn't care about society's expectations at all and the fact that I was still living a life controlled by them hurt my soul.

Things came to a head one day when I spent hours in the library working on a group project to analyze Boeing's growth opportunities. I was baffled by the project. How were we, four college students with no access to inside information at Boeing, supposed to cobble together ways for a multi-billion-dollar company to improve from only articles on the internet? If the company executives and the consulting firms being paid millions of dollars couldn't do it, how would we be able to? Nonetheless, with the habitual automaton-conformity of my past self, I felt a desire to get good grades. So, like an ox at the plow, I continued to pull the load of my education forward, tilling the earth for some unforeseeable future crop to be planted.

There I was in the library at Santa Clara parsing through page after page about airplanes, how they're constructed, where their parts are from, and how they're developed. I started to feel overwhelmed because the more work I did, the more work I realized needed doing. As I dived deeper into the tedium of learning surface-level information about Boeing, my mood grew foul.

Since my Kathunk, I was aware of any lack of authenticity in my actions. As I watched myself work in the library, I started to feel hopeless. My head was aching and spinning at the incredulity of this being all my life was meant to be. I watched myself work towards something I didn't care about just to get a good grade, to be given a stamp of approval by a system of education I didn't even like!

The next few hours were a haze of research and class. I remember nothing about my class except the gray skies and rain falling outside the windows of the room. Finally, late in the afternoon, I was done.

I don't remember leaving the class or what my thoughts were, only my overwhelming hopelessness born from living a life I didn't want to be living. I was conflicted within and could feel it. With my shift in New Zealand, I was now able to fully comprehend how little I cared about what I had been doing for so long. With that comprehension and awareness came a bitter, hopeless darkness beyond every numbness. It was an acute, deep, sharp pain. My inner and outer lives were dissonant, and it *hurt*.

It was February 15th, a Friday afternoon.

I walked on wet sidewalks home from class, under mostly bare trees and gray rain clouds. The rain had turned into a drizzle from the storming wash it had been hours before. Cold, damp air seeped into my bones. The sunlight, blocked by clouds, seemed dim. The weather set the tone for my mood.

As I approached a crosswalk between campus and the road back to my house, I pressed the walk button on the pole of the traffic light and waited, watching cars zoom past me at speeds which seemed faster than they should.

Then, suddenly, a thought came to my mind that I remember word for word, as if carved into my soul: *"You could step in front of those cars and all your suffering would go away."*

I watched the thought come to mind as if time had stopped. The silver Nissan driving by came to a halt, its lights shining through drops of rain, not falling, frozen in time. I watched my breath catch in my chest and my heart stop beating. Then, just as suddenly, I was back.

Rain continued to fall, and I took a firm step away from the road and, thankfully, went on living.

I waited for the light to change and then took my first step onto the road, watching the cars stopped on either side. I realized that I didn't want to die. My body started to shake. I took a few more steps, my mind eerily numb to the world around me, in shock from what it had seen happen. As if coming out of a haze, I found myself another block closer to my house.

Then my brain started to race, analyzing everything that had happened. It went back and sorted through every moment of the experience. I looked down at my hands and found that they were still shaking. I pulled my phone out and called one of my best friends, who I knew had experienced suicidal ideation.

My phone rang once, twice, and then in the middle of the third ring, he picked up. I let out everything that happened as if a dam broke in a cathartic rush of emotions. He listened intently and asked me some questions that I don't remember. He told me he loved me, and we laughed about nothing important. He said to call again if I needed anything and then I hung up.

I walked home and went to my room. I laid down on my bed and stared at my ceiling, as if in a trance. I couldn't believe what my mind had thrown at me. Sure, I was unhappy with my classes and with how I was using my time, but suicide?! Was that really what my brain had come up with as an answer?

As if on cue, my brain rebelled against me and I realized that unless I changed something about how I was living, suicide would be the only answer. Unless I learned to live my life with integrity to my inner knowing, I wouldn't want to live at all. It was a sobering thought at first, but then, as my mind accepted this new commandment, I started to change.

I went to the pits of my own existence on that sidewalk and saw, in full awareness, what waited for me. Where before my Kathunk, I had been swept away by life, letting it live me, after awakening, I had been given agency. Before, I was like a leaf on the wind. After, I was like the wind itself. And as the wind, with full agency over where I went, I had let myself go where I knew I mustn't. I was paying the price. I had let myself experience the pain of actively choosing to live a life that I hated, and the price was not wanting to live.

The next day I wrote in my journal:

I'm so lucky to have had the opportunities I've had, but really that's not the end of it. I'm different from most people and I CAN'T try to force myself to mold into society because I won't mold and bend, I'll break. I don't know what the way forward is from here, but I have to change something. It's crazy how just two months ago I was the happiest I've ever been and now I'm stuck in this shit hole of self-conflict again...

I needed to change but didn't know how to live without molding to society's expectations. I knew who I was, felt whole inside, and had grown my capacity for self-love, but still didn't feel like living. Despite my inner growth, I wanted to die. Despite having people who loved me, I wanted to die. Despite achieving society's version of success for a 20-year-old, I wanted to die. I was missing something crucial.

My moment of suicidal ideation brought me face-to-face with my worst-case scenario: Letting myself actively live a life I didn't want to live. In facing my desire to die, I found a stronger commitment to live right. I decided to never kill myself or waste my life. I decided to turn inside out and bring my full inner self to my outer life.

-11-

INSIDE OUT INTEGRITY

*"The sooner we become less impressed with
our life, our accomplishments, our career, our
relationships, the prospects in front of us—the
sooner we become less impressed and more
involved with these things—the sooner we get
better at them. We must be more than just happy
to be here."*
– MATTHEW MCCONAUGHEY

My story up until this point was one of exploring myself inside. I learned about my soul and my pain by traveling the world and reading books. From here out, my work changed from just inside to aligning my external reality with my internal Truth. Instead of grandiose actions like escaping to Asia, I needed to practice living authentically in every moment. I was still learning how to bring intentionality and authenticity to everyday life. My inner work wasn't done, but my attention needed to shift outside.

Pre-Kathunk, I didn't have a clear idea of what I was living for, but knew I needed to search for something. In New

Zealand, I found my soul. At home, I healed relationships with my parents. But, still, back at Santa Clara, I faced my deepest truth: Despite all my inner growth, without outer alignment, I still didn't want to live. This began the mission to shift my daily life toward an authentic representation of my inner self.

As I made a commitment before to discover my inner Truth, now I committed to bringing that inner Truth out. In my work with clients, there are two parts: The inner journey to find self-love and self-worth and the outer journey to bring that new self into the world. Between the steps is always a rocky transition.

At home, I was the happiest I had ever been and shortly after, I was in the most pain. This was a sign that I was transitioning from part one to part two, from inside to out. Always, just before the end of a journey through the unknown, there is a moment of feeling the most lost. This is the time you most want to give up. Don't. Keep going. Get to the top of the mountain and as the fog lifts, behold the spectacular horizon of your future. Until you heal your inside, the proper view of your outside and your future is obscured. Once you heal inside, your eyes are opened, and you can create whatever outer life you desire. Not until then.

When you see it, everything changes. The work begins again but the type of work shifts. Now, things become easier. Instead of the slog through the mucky swamp of inner trauma and pain, you get to enjoy working hard to climb the mountain. Your legs still burn, and rains still come, but you get to enjoy the views of your life. Now, you get to enjoy doing the work because you know why you're doing it. Before you worked because you had no choice. Now, you work because you choose to. Now your life becomes directed, even if you don't know where it's going. You can see the immediate next step and that's all that matters.

That said, it doesn't happen overnight. This transition between part one and part two lasts forever. The practice of maintaining inner and outer alignment is constant, but a task always worth doing.

In the spring after my headlights moment, I began my practice of inside out living. It was like spring cleaning for my soul. I was a beginner and made many mistakes but had fun in my efforts to live the right way and release the wrong ways.

The first decision I made was to skip more classes that I didn't like. I took 24 units, which for those who don't know is a lot. Instead of giving 100% to all my classes, I routinely skipped my class during lunch. This freed up my time and energy to give more to the classes I liked. For the first time, I started to enjoy school. Because I let go of my ex-self's priorities around grades and universal effort, I was free to be myself. It was a nascent release from "society's" expectations and judgements.

With my alignment of inside and out in daily life, I lived each day differently. I started to enjoy long hours in the library because I was only focusing on what I wanted to learn. I realized that I could use the skills I learned in high school to float by in classes I didn't love in order to try harder in classes I did love. As I brought more authentic intention to my life, I became truly confident for the first time. I was in my element. People took notice.

One day, a woman who sat next to me in my favorite class asked me out on a date. It was the first time anyone had ever asked me out. The class was about two of my favorite subjects, living your dreams and communication. In class, I was on fire, and I knew it. I went into that class excited to learn, participate, and be myself. It was easy to be confident and sure of myself because I loved who I was being.

Being asked out was a big deal because I realized that I was capable of being wanted. I never felt wanted before because I hadn't wanted myself or my life. I didn't like who I was until that spring and so could never feel someone else's affection for me fully.

By healing my trauma and bringing my full inner self to life, I was attractive to someone. After years of rejection and suffering, someone asked me out. Because I had healed, I was able to accept her affection as genuine and enjoy it. I can't emphasize enough how much it meant to be wanted and to be able to feel that appreciation.

She shattered all my stories of not being worthy of love by offering her kindness and affection to me. She showed me genuine affection and appreciation. She showed me that I could be in a healthy relationship. But something felt off. I didn't really think I wanted to be with her forever. I felt myself drifting away. I knew I should tell her and not lead her on, but I was scared to hurt her, so I didn't. In my fear of hurting her, I was still out of Integrity with myself and with her.

Integrity is to have inner and outer alignment with one's Truth. To be aligned with Truth is to do what is right for a person without necessarily understanding why it's right. Truth is not rational, but resonant. We know the truth when it appears, but we don't always understand it. Truth can only be sourced in knowing and feeling, not rationalizing.

Truth is scary because it uncovers fantasy and leaves only reality. Truth is dominant. It will always win every confrontation. All else pales in comparison to the power of Truth. Fantasies crumble when Truth comes. Truth is reality incarnate in our intuition.

In my situation with the girl who asked me out, I wasn't in Integrity with myself or her. By not telling her I wanted to stop seeing her when I realized it, I led her on and I escaped my reality again. I made myself suffer because I wasn't living from Truth.

In my fear of telling her my Truth, I avoided reality and brought myself suffering. I assumed she would hate me when I told her or that I would hurt her. I imagined every possible negative outcome and let myself spiral in anxiety. After months of rumination, I finally told her I just wanted to be friends. She took it well and said she agreed. It was shockingly easy. She wasn't hurt. She didn't hate me. Everything was okay. The fear of speaking my truth and hurting her was much worse than speaking it because it kept me stuck.

This is often the stickiest part of inside out living: The fear of how our true self will be perceived by the outside world. In coaching, I work with all my clients to help them not only uncover their true self and let go of their traumas, but also bring their true selves out into the world.

We are almost all afraid to own our potential to be our greatest selves. When we live from a place of inner truth and show that truth to the outside world, we are being the most vulnerable we can be. When we choose to show the world who we really are, we are risking everything, but still we must do it because if we don't, we will become clogged, the people around us will miss out on our full selves, and we will feel empty again.

Truth allows Life to move forward. Integrity with ourselves and others lets us become who we're meant to be and gives others real ownership of their lives related to us. When we're not in Integrity with ourselves or others, we can't make decisions that are based in reality and neither can the people around us. This keeps everyone involved inside a cycle of suffering.

Integrity is the light that guides us into the unknown. Integrity is the ingredient that allows us to courageously bring our full selves into the world. When we feel that we are being our true selves, it doesn't matter how we're received. This is where courage and confidence come from. When we are in integrity with ourselves, we can be in integrity with others. When we are aligned with integrity, all outcomes are good outcomes. The ripples that come from our true selves are always the ripples that need to come.

-12-

CLEARING THE SLATE

"Follow your bliss and don't be afraid and doors will open where you didn't know they were going to be... The water of immortal life is right there... wherever you are, if you're following your bliss!"
– JOSEPH CAMPBELL

In the summer between my junior and senior years of college, I went to Ghana with the intention to help people and to learn about social entrepreneurship. I was part of a fellowship to help economically empower rural communities in Northern Ghana by assisting them in selling handwoven baskets overseas. As part of our preparation for going abroad, we studied our privilege. Thus, going into the experience, I knew that it was an incredible opportunity that I shouldn't waste.

I was convinced that I found my destiny: Traveling the world and helping poor people live better lives. (This is called being a white savior and is actually pretty messed up.) In Ghana, I quickly realized that dreams aren't always what we expect them to be. Fantasies are not realities; surprise!

Through my months in Ghana, I saw that I didn't love or even like the work of being a social entrepreneur. At first, I was ashamed to admit it. I flew around the globe to work and didn't like it. I was fully funded, yet my work wasn't fulfilling me. I had an impact on the most marginalized people in the world and yet wasn't enjoying my work. It was a privilege but felt like an exhausting effort. I started to understand that even though there was an opportunity to have a real impact in rural Ghana, it wasn't the work for me to do. This was a challenging pill to swallow.

I saw more abject poverty in Ghana than I ever had before: From the cycles of homeless children on the streets of Accra to the illness-stricken families of Bolgatanga. I saw starving children without any access to an escape. I met a nurse who could never live his dream of becoming a doctor because he didn't have access to internet. I saw entire villages with no electricity. Children ate millet with their fingers and mothers begged us for our water. It was a harsh reality. But still, I wasn't inspired.

It made me feel like an evil person. The fact that I could be exposed to so much pain and hardship and still not want to get out of bed in the morning to do something about it killed me.

Even when the weavers we worked with came out of their houses to greet us in dance and song, I couldn't care.

I tried to care, trust me, I tried. But I couldn't. I was only able to live halfheartedly. Every day I wanted to leave. I counted down the days. I hated being in rural Ghana. Despite the real pain around me, I was trapped in my own little world. Every aspect of life rankled me. I missed America. I missed grocery stores and my car. I had constant headaches. Everything felt wrong.

For years I had wanted to be a social entrepreneur working in developing countries to help the people at the margins. For years, I thought it would be my purpose, my passion, my path. But, within days of arriving, I hated my job, I hated my lifestyle, and I hated myself for not loving it. I won a prestigious, fully funded fellowship to go do something good for the world and couldn't get out of bed. What the fuck was I doing?

It was the ultimate slap in the face, the ultimate wakeup call. I dreamed a dream years before of traveling the world to learn about social entrepreneurship. My dream came true, and I didn't want any part in it. Why was that?

At the time, my understanding was messy. I had no clue and felt only frustration and shame. In retrospect, I have learned that not all dreams we hold in our hearts originated there. When I think now of my past self, I see a young man with something to prove. I see someone who, despite his healing, still needed to make an impact to feel worthy. I see someone driven not by an inner calling but by an outer notion of "success." We can always live a prescribed path of success but until we authentically decide for ourselves what is right for us, we will continue to be unfulfilled. The only way to live life rightly is by following what is True, not for others, but for you. At the time, all I knew was that "my" dream had come true, but I was deeply dissatisfied.

At the same time, while the old dreams inside me were dying, they were clearing space for something new. My attachment to prioritizing impact began to dissipate. I started to see that impact can't be the driver or the why because sometimes impact doesn't happen. It's an outcome, not an input.

In Ghana, I watched myself throw away access to an opportunity to impact people because I couldn't rouse my interest. I watched a scenario play out like a gruesome horror film that I hated watching but had to leave on. I watched as I let people starve instead of working hard to help them.

I remember one conversation I had with my mom while I was abroad. I told her how hard it was to be in Ghana and how bad I felt to not be doing more for the people I was there to help. She asked if I could help fund a well or something for a local village. I responded with apathy and explained that I couldn't do that because it's better to empower the locals to help themselves than to give them something like a well. In retrospect, I was making excuses because I felt ashamed. I didn't want to be there or working to help those people and I felt horrible about it.

I was a terrible social entrepreneur in Ghana. I wasn't even a great person there. I tried to force myself to enact a dream that didn't fit me and found that I didn't have any motivation. Simply put, sometimes we cannot do what we are not suited to do. The beaver can't fly, and the eagle can't cut trees down. We cannot do what we cannot do and it's okay.

Looking back, I have slowly learned to forgive myself. I wish I could have given more to those smiling women who danced with us under Baobab and mango trees, but I didn't, and ultimately, what has happened is how it will always be. We must forgive our past selves and learn to grow based on our past shortcomings because we can't change what has already happened.

But still, I resented myself for not being able to do my work. I resented my headaches and blamed them on the weather. I resented the company I worked for and the fellowship team supporting me. I resented the starving people for making me feel bad about myself. I felt an ugly smorgasbord of emotions and tried my best to turn away from them. I didn't understand why I couldn't do my work and felt ashamed, so instead of facing my situation, I escaped into books.

As I escaped from my shame, a beautiful answer started to surface in the words I read. I read about spirituality and purpose, challenges in life, and chosen paths. As much as I tried to escape the answer, somewhere in the twenty books I read, it found me. Finally, I figured it out: It was okay, I was okay. After weeks of resenting myself and the world, it hit me: I didn't have to work as a social entrepreneur in

Ghana to be happy, fulfilled, respected, loved, appreciated, worthy, important. In fact, I could do anything as long as it aligned with who I am! In retrospect, the answer was so obvious, but I couldn't understand it.

It was like a breath of fresh air after a stuffy red eye flight. As I stepped out of the metaphorical plane and into the morning light, I felt refreshed. I had been holding onto this story for so long, thinking it was my dream. My story was that I needed to have the biggest impact for my life to have meaning. In essence, I was still looking for meaning outside myself.

As I came to the realization that I didn't have to save the world or feed the hungry, I was freed to ask myself what I actually wanted. That freedom was more valuable than anything else in the fellowship. As I let go of my grand attachment to solving "the biggest problem," I let go of my lie. The lie was that I needed to solve "the biggest problem" in order to find meaning. The truth I started to see was that there were problems worth solving everywhere, but the bigger truth expanded beyond even that, beyond my comprehension. I only felt the inklings, like having a word stuck on the tip of my tongue.

Going to Ghana was the fulfillment of a dream. The problem, I found, was that the dream wasn't actually mine. As the dream died, my slate cleared of all dreams was now empty. I let go of the lie that meaning comes from impact and found that I could live a meaningful life without "saving the world." But I still didn't know why I was alive. I still hadn't seen beneath the fog of my suffering to my reason for existing. I crossed another thing off the list and was left with one huge problem staring at me: My addiction.

-13-

HEALING ADDICTIONS

"People will do anything, no matter how absurd, to avoid facing their own souls."
– CARL JUNG

Suffering means avoiding our pain and our Truth. Suffering means choosing to live in a liminal, in-between space where there is no meaning except the perpetuation of one's suffering. Most of us are exposed to pain as children and all of us are exposed to more throughout our lives. We transform these pains into trauma when we don't face them and eventually accumulate layers and layers of trauma. Until we heal and get to our core traumas, we suffer. Until we face our pain, we avoid it. In order to avoid our pain, we use external distractions, which we become addicted to.

My external distraction, my addiction, was porn, or, at a deeper level, sexuality. There are several main things that I've found people are addicted to today: Sex, money, drugs, self-harm, power, food, TV, social media, video games, work, exercise, books, and self-loathing. This isn't an exhaustive list. People can be addicted to anything that allows them to avoid their pain and their reality or to cling to their non-reality.

I started watching porn at age 11 because I was curious, but quickly curiosity became reliance. I came to rely on porn to make me numb to my pain. When I felt sad, alone, misunderstood, frustrated, unloved, or even bored, I turned to porn.

From age 12 to 19, I watched porn almost every day. I saw horrible images and videos that no one should be exposed to. I became so desensitized to the horror that it bored me, and I sought out even more damaging content to watch in order to feel anything at all.

Watching porn was like sexually harassing myself every day. Some people might not understand this or think that I'm exaggerating. I'm not. What I saw and what was normalized for me scarred me, perhaps forever. At 11, my brain was still forming and so porn literally changed my mind. I became desensitized to things like rape and assault. I became desensitized to whether sexuality was between real people or if it was animated animals. I watched robots have sex with people. I saw horrors, I promise you.

As I write this, I feel like puking. It's so horrible to remember what it was like to subject myself to the horrors of porn. After watching, I always felt like a piece of shit. I felt like I shouldn't be alive and that I didn't deserve love. And yet I went back to it because I couldn't face my deeper pain.

The definition of an addiction is something bad for us that we can't stop doing. We all have them. It's simple self-destruction. We all do it all the time. Sometimes it's as simple as eating a few too many bites (or pints) of Ben and Jerry's. Other times it's getting fucked up on 16 drinks, stumbling to a cold beach at night, and hooking up with someone you barely know. I've been through the wringer, and it isn't pretty.

Addiction isn't nice to talk about, write about, or read about. It's ugly and foul. It's slimy and gross. It makes us hate ourselves under the guise of protecting us. It's horrible, yet we must shine the light on it. Despite the shame and aversion we feel toward our addictions and the addictions of others, we must open up about them. We must be vulnerable.

We have a culture that is addicted to all manners of painkillers. We avoid pain like the plague. We avoid our inner work above all else because it scares us. When we keep quiet about our addictions, we're perpetuating this suffering society. When we avoid hearing people when they share with us about their shame and addiction, we avoid giving ourselves the opportunity to heal.

For eight years, I watched porn without ever wanting to stop. I didn't tell anyone about it. I didn't want to. Somewhere inside, I knew that if I opened up about it, people would judge me and that would make me confront my shame and inner pain. Early in college, I finally opened up about it to a friend. Just like I was expecting, the first people I shared with, told me to stop. I resented them for telling me to give up porn. I resented them for thinking that they knew me better than I knew myself. At first, I refused to listen, obstinate in my suffering.

It wasn't until I lost the opportunity to do something important to me that I listened. Porn made it so that I couldn't have sex with real women. I had desensitized my brain so thoroughly to reality, that it only responded to fantasies. I didn't feel like I could have a real relationship because my body didn't respond to the women I cared about. The first time I discovered this, I was 18. But still, it took me another three years to quit.

It wasn't until New Zealand that I earnestly tried to stop watching porn for the first time. I don't have much memory of porn or of trying to quit. It's all covered under the fog of my suffering. But I remember trying. I used habit tracker apps to count my consecutive sober days. I got to a few weeks before relapsing. I tried blocking porn on my computer, but always found a way around the walls I made for myself. My addiction was devious and subversive. It made me think that I was in control all while weakening my discipline so that at the first sign of my inner darkness, I could escape.

By the time I went to Ghana in the summer of 2019, I had been trying to quit porn for almost two years. I had some longer stretches and some shorter ones, but I hadn't managed to give it up entirely. In Ghana, I watched porn (for what I thought would be) the last time. I remember the feeling I got after watching it of complete self-loathing. I hated myself for doing something so hurtful, not only to myself but to others.

I knew that the porn industry was messed up and that it perpetuated misogyny, sexual assault, child sex trafficking, and other awful things. I knew how horrible it was and how bad it made me feel. I knew it, but until that last time, I didn't feel it. The last time, I felt so disgusted with myself and so full of self-hate that I vowed to never watch it again.

I'm open about my addiction and people often ask me how I quit. I never know quite what to say. There were so many different variables that gave me the courage to stop. If not for the inner healing work, I wouldn't have been able to quit. If not for the level of understanding I had about the pain porn caused others, I wouldn't have been able to quit. If not for the years of effort I had put into trying already, I wouldn't have been able to quit.

But the hardest part about addictions isn't quitting, it's staying quit. When we inevitably relapse, we must love ourselves anyway. Since I wrote this chapter the first time, after two years without porn, I relapsed. There is shame and there is blame but the lesson is love. When we fall out of integrity with ourselves, especially with something important like conquering an addiction, it's most important to give ourselves love in order to stay in the light. Only from the light can we let it burn away the shame and guilt of being fallible humans.

Addictions come to us as distractions from our pain and trauma. We throw ourselves into self-destructive habits so that we can feel something that isn't numbness. We desperately try to avoid going inside and dealing with ourselves. To overcome addiction, we must first overcome ourselves by going inside and cleaning our traumas. We must learn to love ourselves with all our scars. We must forgive ourselves for the mistakes we've made. We must allow ourselves space to be perfectly imperfect. Only from a place of true self love can we cease self-destruction.

Even still, remain vigilant. Once addicted, always addicted. Accept that you are the way you are and love yourself anyway. If you relapse, love yourself anyway. If you don't, love yourself anyway. Always, always, always come from a place of divine, full self-love when dealing with addictions, because more than anything else, addictions are the opposite of self-love. Addictions are the darkness where love is the light. To conquer them, you must shine brighter than their darkness.

Cultivate your capacity to love yourself by telling yourself, "I love you" every day, every hour, every minute. Do loving kindness meditations. Write affirmations. Do every cheesy thing that you need to do to find self-love because only from self-love can you find the true awe of being alive. Only from self-love can you enjoy your life. Love yourself!

If you're struggling with any kind of addiction, know that you can beat it. No matter what it is, you can beat it. You are powerful. It won't be easy, and it might take years, but you can do it. It took me ten years to conquer my addiction the first time. After two years without porn, I relapsed but the journey I've taken to the land of self-love and fulfillment makes it okay. I'm not controlled by porn anymore. Even if I relapse, I don't let it dictate my self-worth anymore. I've built practices of self-care that guard my heart from my old addictions and shame.

The best way to free ourselves from shame is to open up and be vulnerable. When we expose our shame through vulnerability, we let the love and light of those around us assist us in letting go of the shame to see the pain underneath.

A year and half after quitting porn in Ghana, I posted on Instagram a photo of my habit tracking app showing hundreds of days without porn. It was one of the scariest things I had ever done, and I did it not for myself but for others. I knew that there were people out there suffering, watching porn, and not feeling seen or known. I knew that they needed to have an opportunity to open up about porn, so I created the space even though I was scared shitless.

When I posted the photo and some paragraphs about why I posted it, I started to shake. I was so scared to be vulnerable about something so close to my heart that my body shook. I threw my phone across my room onto the bed and went outside for a walk. As I walked, I told myself I had done the right thing, that people need to see vulnerability to be vulnerable. But the voices of my doubts surfaced too: People will see how horrible you are and hate you forever.

A bit much, right?

When I got back home, I opened my phone to find over 50 messages from friends telling me how courageous I had been and how inspired they were by my vulnerability. It was awe-inspiring and made me feel connected to people I almost never spoke to. Over the next months, people came up to me in the halls at school and messaged me on Instagram asking for advice about quitting. It was so validating and gratifying that my courage and vulnerability could lead to impact on others. Not only did it help others, though, it also helped me.

When I posted about porn, I lost some of the shame associated with it. By showing my imperfect self to the world, I accepted my imperfections and my addictions. By accepting myself, my shame had nowhere to live, and I could finally be free of its burden. Shame is a tool of addiction to control us. When I quit porn, I began my journey of letting go of shame, but it has been exactly that, a journey. Shame is powerful and doesn't ever leave us completely.

An Intermission

EMPTY OF PAIN

PHEW! That was a heavy one, huh?! Take some breaths, go outside, make a smoothie. Relax and percolate.

Though things were still hard after Ghana, I was open to pain again, and the hardness became different. Instead of escaping from my pain into addiction, I faced it head on and learned from it. This changed everything. I no longer suffered by avoiding truth but felt the repercussions of my actions and adjusted course. I chose to learn and grow instead of avoiding what was too painful.

That being said, I certainly wasn't (and am not) perfect, so sometimes I still avoided the truth. But the key difference was when things inevitably went badly, I didn't run away from my mistakes as I had in the past. I accepted them and let myself feel the repercussions. It wasn't comfortable, but it was much easier than the deep revulsion I felt toward myself when I was suffering. The truth is scary, but it is also the key to unlocking a life of adventure, exploration, and joy because only from truth can we grow.

Part 4 of this book was the hardest to write for me because it required me to face the ugliest parts of myself head on. It required me to confront my shame and self-doubt and choose myself. If you have read this far, maybe you have some resistance to finishing the book. Maybe you're uncomfortable with the details I shared about my life. But this is exactly why I wrote this book: to help you confront the most uncomfortable parts of your life and your story. Remember that vulnerability is the antidote for shame and once cured life becomes an adventure once more.

PART 5
THE BEAUTY BENEATH

AWE

"

Out beyond ideas of wrongdoing and rightdoing,
there is a field. I'll meet you there.
When the soul lies down in that grass,
the world is too full to talk about.
Ideas, language, even the phrase "each other"
doesn't make any sense.
The breeze at dawn has secrets to tell you.
Don't go back to sleep.
You must ask for what you really want.
Don't go back to sleep.
People are going back and forth across the doorsill
where the two worlds touch.
The door is round and open.
Don't go back to sleep.

"

— RUMI

-14-

FUNGI EQUALS FUN GUY

*"The mystical journey seems to offer a graduate
education in the obvious."*
– MICHAEL POLLAN

As a child, I went to Flying Deer Nature Camp every summer. I met my lifetime best friends there. I learned about wild edibles and how to camouflage myself by slathering mud all over my body. I played games and honed my senses. I snuck through brambles and ran across the earth. I carved sticks and marveled at simple treasures of nature. I learned how to create fire from what I found in the woods and how to build shelters to sleep in. I was one with the Earth and unquestionably present with life.

As I aged, I lost this presence and appreciation for nature. I was mired down by the worries and ruminations of a young adult. How will I do well in school? How can I find love? What job will I get after I graduate? Where will I live? What's important to me? What am I here for? Why am I alive? The sorts of questions that haunt us every day.

Then, in the summer of 2019, home in New England, I ate some "magic" mushrooms, and my life changed forever. Before I dive into this life-changing experience, I must explain the history of psychedelics and where the ubiquitous vilification of these substances comes from.

Psychedelics have gotten a bad rap in our society because of years of misuse and misinformation. Various psychoactive medicines have been used by native healers for thousands of years to serve people with all sorts of problems from relationships to physical pain. In the 50s, psychedelics came to the US for the first time. Many different universities studied their efficacy to treat various mental health issues and addictions. They found some early success but then in the 70s, Nixon began the war on drugs, not to help people, but to maneuver politically.

A quote from John Ehrlichman, who served as Nixon's domestic policy chief encapsulates this sentiment: "The Nixon campaign in 1968, and the Nixon White House after that, had two enemies: the antiwar left and black people. You understand what I'm saying. We knew we couldn't make it illegal to be either against the war or black, but by getting the public to associate the hippies with marijuana and blacks with heroin, and then criminalizing both heavily, we could disrupt those communities. We could arrest their leaders, raid their homes, break up their meetings, and vilify them night after night on the evening news. Did we know we were lying about the drugs? Of course we did." The history of drug legality in our country is rife with racism and lies.

Psychedelics became another part of this "war on drugs" and were vilified with propaganda throughout the last 50 years. Over the last 10 years or so, marijuana has become legalized in many states in the US and life goes on. Psychoactive truffles are legal recreationally in the Netherlands and life goes on. My point is not to say that there aren't dangers and risks of using these substances, but to say that the dangers and risks aren't as magnified as Nixon and the following administrations might have led us to believe. The dangers of using psychedelics pale in comparison to other legal substances like alcohol and nicotine.

There are risks of using psychedelics, but with the right preparation, set/setting, dosage, and integration these substances can lead to deepening one's connection to the beauty and joy of being alive without major risk.

I planned my first trip extensively. When thinking about the risks involved, I first learned about Set and Setting, or your mind(set) and your physical (setting). Set is everything going on inside you and setting is everything going on outside you.

Common wisdom says to start with a low dose for one's first psychedelic experience and work up to higher doses if desired on following trips. Keep all ego and competition out of this; psychedelics are not like beers and there's nothing cool about consuming the most.

I set aside three full days for my experience without any obligations or commitments. Before my trip, I journaled and set intentions. After my trip, I took time to write about and reflect on what happened. Most importantly, I made time to integrate the experience even up to months and years later. Without integration, there is no purpose to doing psychedelics. Their gift comes from their astounding ability to create lasting change outside of the experience, but that only happens with integration.

Finally, before I get into the story, you should know that these substances should not be used by everyone, they are not a panacea, and they are not literally magic. They are sacred and to be respected but not feared. I am not recommending anyone do these substances, only sharing my experiences of doing them. The world is changing, and legality will change with it, but remember these substances are illegal. Okay, into the story.

I set up a plan to be in the best environment for my well-being. I knew I needed people I trusted around me to keep me safe, a forest that I was familiar with, a fire, and a summer day. I decided to have my experience at a friend's land.

It was morning, maybe 7:30 am. I took out my mushrooms, which smelled of earth and dirt and looked like shriveled, dry, brown finger-bones. I brewed them into tea, added lemon, and then drank the rather yucky concoction. The mushrooms had become chewy and so I mashed them around my mouth and finally swallowed everything down.

I made sure to have two of my best friends spend the day trip-sitting me. I asked them to both be sober in order to provide me support for the day. One of them had prior experience with psychedelics and knew how to keep my conscious mind from freaking out by reminding me of what I already knew: These substances can't kill you and any experience is temporary. With that support and the freedom to experience anything, we walked outside to light a fire. It was a beautiful summer morning as the sun rose over fields of vibrant green grass and waving trees.

We performed a ceremony from our childhood and spoke our intentions for the experience. I was the only one taking mushrooms. I had two trip-sitters, both of whom I trusted immensely. I knew my environment well and felt safe and at home. I had a few nerves going into the experience but was mostly just excited. My intention was to be open to any experience. Mushrooms often give us exactly what we need but that we didn't know we needed. My trip was no different.

For years and years, I overthought everything. I ruminated about life and my problems endlessly. Because I overthought everything, all my lows turned into spirals and all my highs never fully happened. I wasted years of my life stuck in my head without actually living. I had experienced many gifts in life only to let them turn into burdens due to overthinking, rumination, and inaction. Four hours on mushrooms changed my understanding of how we can choose to think and exist forever.

The first thing I remember about my experience was feeling unusually light, both weightless and light-like, brighter.

The second thing I remember was the rightness of the experience. I had only experienced weed and alcohol before mushrooms. Doing mushrooms felt completely different. Where alcohol and weed (sometimes) took me out of reality, mushrooms brought me into the presence of reality. I had perfect clarity with everything around me. I felt totally lucid, as if seeing the world for the first time with a clear vision. Everything was different, more real.

I looked at my best friend's mom who was about 60. Her hair was so white, and her skin looked like a gnarled old tree. I saw every line in her skin. I thought that she looked ancient, like she would blow away in the breeze. And yet, I saw fortitude and strength in her. I saw her power as she broke branches to feed the fire and I saw her inner resilience. I was awed by her in a way that I hadn't experienced before. I felt so much joy and gratitude for her being alive and for the elders in my life. I had my camera out and took a photo of her, in all her furrowed and ancient beauty. I noticed her mortal nature.

The trip helped me see that my loved ones wouldn't live forever. I realized that everyone is dying and being re-born constantly and saw the importance of accepting and appreciating people for who they are right now. Beyond people, I realized that how things are in the moment will never be how things are again and that each moment is dying just as it is born. The present moment is a beautiful, fleeting thing, but only in the present moment can we exist. So, freedom, fulfillment, joy, meaning, are all found right now, always.

It's important to mention that doing psychedelics showed me great Truths like this one, but they didn't integrate those truths into my life. That was work I had to do later. While I was tripping, I got it, but after, I didn't. It was like having a memory of getting it without understanding it at all. After every experience on psychedelics, I've had to do the sober work to understand and integrate the lessons into my life. It hasn't always been easy or happened quickly.

After our fire, I got my camera and sought out beauty. I walked around, more confident than I ever had been, not knowing an alternative to confidence. I just existed without the capacity for self-doubt. I had no thoughts or inner monologue. I acted on instinct alone. I walked from plant to plant and took photos of the minutia: Seeds and flower petals. Colors became brighter at the fringes and edges of objects. My sight blurred into pink and green dots. The world was so brilliant, so vibrant.

We wandered into the woods. The sun was hot but not too hot. On the way into the woods, we passed a field of goldenrod stalks reaching staunchly into the sunshine, waving orbs of fuzz at us. I looked at them and immediately had the urge to run into the goldenrod. I rushed forward, scattering the stalks and hiding inside the grasses. I was like a child again, back at camp, playing in the woods.

Back on the path and as we walked into the woods, I became aware of where the sun transitioned to shadow. As we walked under the canopy, the sun went from drenching to dappling the earth. I laid down in the middle of the shadow and light and looked up at the sky, knowing that I was between two worlds, at an entrance point to the great forest beyond. Much life is in the great forest, beyond the borders of light and darkness.

I started to find treasures. I found a huge turkey feather, a weird red plant that dripped sticky blood-like-stuff when I ripped it open, and a bright red maple leaf. I found lots of things to treasure in the moment but was happy to give them back to nature for they were not mine. I realized that what I own is not mine, I am simply borrowing it from mother earth for a time. I learned that I don't need to be attached to things for they will return to the earth anyway. Again, I knew this lesson at the time without doubt, but would have to relearn the lesson again later as a sober self.

In the real woods, off the path, I ran into the forest with bare feet. I jumped over logs and brushed past branches. I ripped heavy rocks out of the ground and threw them with all my might. I broke rotten tree trunks and toppled them over. I climbed trees, totally aware of my body and in control of every movement. I turned into an animal and was totally in my body. I realized how amazing my body was. I was in awe of what I could do. Everything was so easy and natural. My body was as it was for animals, a powerful vessel to carry, to run, to climb, to break, and to hold. For a time, I had no thoughts, only instincts.

Each part of my body was unique and yet attached to the same whole. As I slowed down and invited my friends to walk back toward the house with me, I had a thought, which seemed totally natural. The voice of self-judgement in my mind was completely absent and I felt totally comfortable to say anything that came to my mind.

So, without thinking about it, I said: "My toes are the same as my tongue." My friends looked at me and then burst out laughing. Then I was laughing with them. I heard myself say it and knew from some past self's experience of life that it was a ridiculous thing to say. Yet, I couldn't shake the feeling that I knew what I was talking about. Our bodies are whole things, just as all things are whole. Our hands are part of the greater body just as we are part of the greater existence of life. Toward the end of my trip, I wrote:

Today I didn't care what people thought of me and I was happy to just be. I felt like my shell was gone, evaporated as if it went from solid to liquid and then to gas. I still noticed that people might think things about me, but I didn't care, at least not as much. I didn't want to be mean, but also, I didn't hold back. I like who I am when I say what I think/feel/want...

I feel as if I have grown but perhaps I have grown for the wrong reasons into something/one I am not meant to be. I should not grow because of what others tell me because then I will grow into something that I have been shaped to be. The only way to truly grow and flourish as my own unique self is to listen to my heart and be who I am. What I found today is that it is natural to be myself if I just slip into it—if I slip into who I am with ease and be lucid.

This experience on shrooms was another awakening moment in my life. Because I had done so much work to heal my psyche, I eased into the shrooms experience. I was healthy and prepared. My experience was not challenging, but beautiful. It took me out of my mind and put me into my body. It showed me death and life up close and reminded me to be present. It brought me back to my childhood and taught me to have fun with life by getting out of rumination. It wasn't what I expected, but it was what I needed. It opened me to a life lived without doubt or rumination and showed me the beauty of being me. That being said, integration always takes work.

-15-

BROKEN OPEN

*"The wound is the place where the Light
enters you."*
– RUMI

Immediately after returning to Santa Clara for the fall
of my senior year, I fell in love and had my heart broken.
Within the span of three months, I rode a relationship roll-
ercoaster from highest highs to lowest lows. This was the
first time in my life I had ever fallen for someone who also
fell for me and there was nothing quite like it.

It happened like a tinder bundle being blown into life,
slowly at first with smoke and tears, and then all at once
hot like the desert sun, so hot it must be thrown down,
then burned to a crisp. It came and went in the blink of
an eye. Yet the relationship lit a greater fire and served its
purpose as the catalyst for something to come by dying in
the process.

My first real love came to me as a surprise. With
the sweet innocence of youth, I fell. Like a flower bloom-

ing in spring, I came alive with vibrancy and passion. I didn't mean to fall in love, but I guess that's why they call it falling.

It was sudden, abrupt, and intense. I felt drawn in, as if after a cliffhanger. Each moment brought me further along, tantalizing, dramatic, beautiful, painful.

She and I had been friends for years and had crossed paths here and then, smiling and growing closer, but still not close. One day, we went hiking with a third friend and I was drawn in.

The three of us climbed up a mountain, through the crispy, yellow grasses of late summertime in California. We walked over the rocks of dried riverbanks and under trees hung with Spanish moss catching the light of early afternoon sunshine. I built up a sweat and pushed up the hill, starting to feel my legs burn and my heart open.

I noticed each time that she and I made eye contact. When she caught my eye or I caught hers, I looked at her with an intensity I couldn't control. It was like laser vision, burning desire into her soul, communicating through our eyes, without words to understand what was being shared. I didn't mean to feel my feelings, but feel them I did.

That day we went on our first date. It was wonderful. We improvised lyrics to songs we made up, drank blueberry beer, and sat by the river. We kissed beneath the afternoon sun and the giggles of new connection gurgled like the river nearby. All was well.

As time went on, we went on more dates. We brought dinner and wine to the beach for sunset, skinny dipped in the waves, and lay in the cold sand beneath a tapestry of stars. I read her books beneath the sun, and she played me Bob Dylan. I watched her flowing hair shine in the wind as her fingers wove patterns of sound on the guitar. It was beautiful and delicious like a bouquet of chocolate roses. Yet with every rose, there is a thorn, and sometimes many.

I brought two thorns into the relationship that would lead to its inevitable end.

Thorn one: Since childhood, I struggled to accept love from people because I felt unworthy of being loved and this led to a fear of losing her. Because I was afraid to lose her, I tried to spend as much time with her as possible. Subconsciously, I wanted to prove to myself that someone who I wanted would want me for me. It was a vicious cycle: The more fun we had together, the more attached I became and then the more I clung to her for meaning.

This is where the real trouble began. When I started to escape from my own life into seeking validation from her, I lost track of my purpose, of my own journey and put all the pressure of my life onto her. I can't know what that was like for her, but I imagine it was challenging and felt unfair. I imagine that when I got upset that she was busy working on things she cared about, she felt like I didn't care about her.

Distance started to form between us as she felt pressured to be in something much more serious than it was. As the distance formed, I clung even harder. I wrote letters and poems, songs and notes. I did everything I could to keep her because I was scared to lose my own source of meaning. It wasn't fair to her, and it wasn't fair to me. I wasn't giving myself enough credit as a human being with passions and goals. I let my healing path fall apart because I found an external source of direction and meaning.

Eventually, the second metaphorical thorn poked me and drew my blood. For years, I hadn't been able to get hard with women because porn changed the neural pathways in my brain and made it much more challenging to react to real women in "normal" ways. Many young men struggle with erectile dysfunction but it's such a taboo subject that we don't talk about it. Where there are taboos, there is shame and under the shame there is often fear. For me, beneath the shame was the fear of not being good enough for the woman I fell for. I thought that if I couldn't get hard with her, I didn't deserve to be with her.

One night, we were lying in bed together and we decided to try to have sex. I was confident that it would work. I felt attracted to her and excited by the concept, but as soon as I got a condom out, I got soft. At that moment, she turned over and started to cry. I felt awful. I felt like a complete and utter failure of a human being. All I wanted to do was give love to the person I cared about in the way they asked for, in the way that was expected of people our age, and I couldn't.

Over the next month, we drifted apart, came back together, and then ruptured. We stopped talking. I felt hurt and betrayed. She told me that she felt hurt and betrayed.

Neither of us came out of our relationship feeling good about it... and yet I think we both were better because it happened. I learned a lot about myself, about relationships, and about what not to do. I learned how to communicate and how to listen. She taught me these things and for that I am grateful.

What we had was beautiful, painful, and sweet. When it broke, the shattering of my heart rang deep, but that pain gave way to healing and to gratitude. It broke me so cleanly open that I saw straight to my core, to all my insecurities, and to my deepest shame. In my broken shambles, I had the opportunity to understand my heart fully and to put myself back together, leaving behind the old stories and insecurities that didn't serve me anymore. I received the gift of healing that comes from heartbreak.

In the midst of my breaking, I took a trip to the Sierra Nevada mountains. I walked into the woods listening to music. It was late and the stars were glorious. As I walked away from my campsite, I started to cry, the sounds of *Helplessly Hoping* in my ears. As one song turned into the next, Neil Young sang *Harvest Moon* to me, and I laid my body down in the dirt and stared at the stars above. I was overcome by racking sobs and, for a short while, was unable to be anything but broken.

But, as I cried, something magical happened. All the heaviness of the breakup, all my shame about my body, all my insecurities about finding love and being abandoned rose from me like ghosts to join the stars. Every tear made me feel lighter and lighter until I was giggling uncontrollably in the dirt in the middle of nowhere in the Sierras. I was healing my heart and letting go of my need for external sources of love.

Eventually, I would discover words for what I was experiencing from Anthony De Mello. Those words go like this: "You become happy not being loved, not being desired by or attractive to someone. You become happy by contact with reality. That's what brings happiness, a moment by moment contact with reality." We shared moments of real beauty, but through it all, under the surface, I was aware that it wasn't right. Despite my knowing, I pushed through it because I wanted to believe that it was right. I chose fantasy over reality and in doing so, suffering over pain. But, the pain came anyway, as it always will, when the truth finally hit me.

In conversations with my clients and friends, I often hear the disappointment that comes from avoiding Truth in relationships. When we avoid the Truth in other areas of life, we are left suffering and alone. When we avoid the Truth in relationships, we suffer alone and so does the other person. In avoiding the Truth, we are choosing mutual, isolated suffering. Yet many people do just this because owning the pain of needing to speak Truth is too frightening.

I succumbed to fear in my relationship when I refused to see Truth. This made me blame her for my emotions. I gave away ownership of my life and sought fulfillment from her. When my heart broke it was because I realized that this will never, ever work and that I needed to create my own fulfillment and not rely on another person.

Relationships are beautiful things. Romance is fun and filled with joy. Yes, partners can bring us happiness and even real meaning, but they cannot be the ultimate source of meaning. If meaning is sourced from outside a person it will always, always eventually stop coming.

It's impossible to find true meaning and fulfillment from something outside of one's self. When we feel fulfilled from something it's because it aligns with our deepest desires. When a person has a child, they find fulfillment in raising that child not because of the child but because of their calling to have and raise kids. When people are fulfilled by their work, it's not because of the outcome of their work, but because they're doing the work that they're meant to be doing in the world. Meaning comes from inside, always.

Relationships with others do bring joy and meaning, but only when we are in them for the right reasons.

When our deepest desires are in alignment with the reality that we are creating for ourselves, we find fulfillment. When we look outside ourselves and avoid Truth, fulfillment is impossible. There is a difference between creating a desired reality and escaping a painful reality into a desired fantasy. In this difference, is all a person needs to know to live a fulfilling life. When we seek fantasy because it is easier or more alluring, we deny ourselves True joy and meaning.

I put so much pressure on our relationship to bring me fulfillment that I stifled the small spark we had at the beginning. It made me think about how many times I'd done this in the past. Over and over, I fell in love with the idea of a person and put all my hopes onto that facade. By creating a fantasy version of someone, I put pressure on them to be that person, I buried them in the weight of my fantasies. That's not fair to them, nor to me. The only person who should bear the weight of my dreams is me.

The problem was that I didn't know how to carry my own dreams, they were too overwhelming, too huge. My dreams scared me, so I ran away from them, looking outside myself for spiritual sustenance. I fled my dreams into fantasies and in the process lost a friend. It was a painful and important lesson for me, one that I continue to learn, still. It takes years to integrate lessons into ourselves. Be patient and move forward anyway.

From inside my broken heart, I found a valuable truth: I couldn't find fulfillment outside myself and needed to create my own meaning.

-16-

SNOW MELT

"And you would accept the seasons of your heart,
even as you have always accepted the seasons that
pass over your field. And you would watch with
serenity through the winters of your grief. Much of
your pain is self-chosen."
– KHALIL GIBRAN

Despite realizing powerful truths, my heart was still breaking open. The entrance into 2020 was filled with a discovery of deep pain. Within that pain was a powerful beauty.

I had learned that meaning in life needs to come from within but struggled to embody the idea. Even as my brain led me in a revolution, my heart played catch up. I sat in my sadness, enjoying most of life but always coming back to my feelings of loss. I didn't know how to move forward or grow through my sadness.

I want to clarify: In this time of low and slow, I wasn't suffering in the way I did when I was younger. Until my

Kathunk moment in New Zealand, I was suffering because I wasn't letting myself feel my painful, scary emotions. Between New Zealand and my breakup, I was able to feel pain and resolve my traumas.

Now, I was experiencing something different: sadness. It took me a while to understand the difference. This sadness and grief was something new. It was happening in the present moment. Where my suffering and pain were both attached to the past, sadness was current.

It was as if, over the years of resolving my pain and trauma, I emptied most of my old, untouched pains and made room for new pain to take root. Except, in this new version of me, I was able to see my pain in real time and had the capacity for self-love, so I could embrace it and welcome it in without trying to avoid reality. My sadness came from meeting reality as it was for me in the moment.

This was something I was unable to do until after my relationship ended. In my relationship, I sought meaning outside myself and was attached to someone's validation of me. In the pain of healing my broken heart, I slowly let go of that need and my old pain so that I could exist in the present moment.

The quality of the feeling brought me down, but it felt different than any feeling I had experienced before. When I felt grief about my relationship ending it was painful, but my pain came and went, rather than staying, and something amazing started to happen. Even as I felt sad, I started to laugh, like in the Sierras but every day. With every bout of tears came joy. It was as if by emptying myself of tears and letting myself feel the reality of my experience, I was gifted with fresh joyfulness. Like in the Sierras, letting myself feel my true pain opened me up to joy.

That winter, I was home in Massachusetts and decided to go for a walk in the wintery wonderland. It was my first, solo winter walk in the woods of the season. I walked under trees, their branches weighed down with snow and over crunchy, crispy, snow-covered earth. I felt snow fall in my face. It was silent except for the sound of my boots on the path. If I stopped, there was nothing. It was blissful. When I returned home, I wrote:

It seems that every time I come back to the cold, I have to reacquaint myself with it. I always begin the process like one would the stages of grief, with denial. I deny the cold entry into myself, refusing to lower my warm self into the depths of the freeze. I linger in defiant disbelief that such a thing could exist. Every time I come back to winter, I have to relearn that it is normal, perfectly normal.

From denial I continue into some mishmash of pain, anger, and blame of those around me and of myself. I succumb to the cold, let it take hold of my heart and wrap its knobby, long, freezing fingers around me. I seek out those around me to take the burden, to let me avoid those feelings that I know are coming. I long to be released from the dismal darkness even in my denial that I must feel at all.

Then, the truth starts to seep in as I begin to thaw. The ice that has caressed the edges of my soul starts to melt and with it my heart's beat can once more begin to sound out its cry. I realize that inside the pain, anger, and blame is sadness. These outward emotions are always a sign for me of something inside that I haven't dealt with or that I have been reminded of but haven't noticed. With this realization, I can cry and with the tears of the thaw come the floods and the flowers.

Finally, it is spring, the heaviness of the snow has departed leaving only muddied walkways to work through. My feet are sucked into the earth with each step. Yet, faithfully, I walk forward because I can feel the coming warmth. In springtime I can look back toward the departing winter and realize that it brought with it growth, renewal, and rest; that even in the cold, on the darkest of days, there is life... Under the snow, lie seeds and sprouts just waiting to burst through towards the sun.

In the blink of an eye another winter has come and gone, another voyage of the heart has been completed, into the depths and out again. Winter never seeks to cause harm, only to remind us of what lies inside, under the snow on our hearts. As the sun comes once again, I realize that winter is perhaps the most magical time of all. Sometimes only in the darkness, can we find the most important light.

And breathe. Find stillness. Sometimes only in the darkness, can we find the most important light.

Breathe into that. Let it wash over you. Let it cleanse you of your shame and open you to forgiveness. What a beautiful sentiment.

Welcome to beauty.

-17-

MY MAGNOLIA

"Trees are sanctuaries. Whoever knows how to
speak to them, whoever knows how to listen to
them, can learn the truth. They do not preach
learning and precepts, they preach, undeterred by
particulars, the ancient law of life."
– HERMANN HESSE

One spot, more than all others in the entire world, holds a place in my heart. It is where I found my God, my spiritual direction, peace, and beauty. It is a spot of such profound grace. This spot is under a Magnolia tree in the Mission Gardens at Santa Clara University. Imagine this:

You arrive flying around one building and then the next at ninety-degree angles on your longboard and a spectacular sight opens in front of you. The first thing you notice are the roses blooming in all different colors from yellow to purple and everything in between. The second thing you see are palm trees and the one towering willow-like gargantuan tree with shimmering leaves. The third thing you notice as you take another smooth turn on your board is a bench settled beneath a perfect magnolia tree covered in pink blossoms.

Then, before you see them, you smell springtime in your lungs, like the sweet and gentle kiss of a new lover. The smell is like nothing else. It's sweet like honey and when added to the loam, roses, Magnolia blossoms, and dirt is like caramelized earth. You see them: hundreds and thousands of tiny purple wisteria blossoms hanging on vines from old, wooden arches. To complete the vision, the sun is shining, the wind is blowing a cool breeze on a hot day, and you are utterly at peace.

That is my bench. My, oh my, do I love my bench, my magnolia tree, my Aleph[3].

I described my bench in springtime, as I best remember it, but here I want to share a story not from spring but autumn.

I was sitting at my bench late in the fall of 2019 reading the concluding story in a series of books about war, love, magic, and faith. I was overcome by gratitude. As I turned the last page, I looked up to see the sun shining through the leaves in the tree above me. The winds came gently, caressing the leaves, tantalizing them to fall and fall they did, tenderly weaving to the earth. The throes of their last dying life force, in full view for me. I was overcome by the immensity of goodness in the world, as it is inherently just so. The beauty of the leaves falling hauntingly to the ground to feed a new spring touched my soul. I looked to

[3]Read the book, by Paolo Coelho and google the word in Jewish Mysticism.

the west and saw the sun fall behind the branches of a tall evergreen tree. The sun spread its rays of light all around it, as it does only when half hidden. I leapt off the bench and climbed to the top of the magnolia tree.

At the top, the sun was still in full force. I climbed beyond the shade of the horizon into the lingering warmth. As I sat in the tree, the wind swaying me back and forth, I felt pressed to close my eyes and pray. I had never prayed, and it was profoundly unfamiliar, yet as I did, I felt only peace. I am not religious and never have been, but as I closed my eyes and felt the sun and the wind, heard the rush of the breeze, smelled the decomposing earth below, I was touched by an energy. All negativity was expelled from me, and I was so full of gratitude for my life, the highs and the lows. I prayed to my own heart and to the energy I felt, offering surrender in return for guidance. I heard a call.

As I swung down from the tree, I closed my eyes once more and returned to the feeling of peace and warmth emanating both from within and all around me. I allowed myself to feel guided in a direction, gently continuing my surrender. I remembered that when I was younger, I used to do the same thing, always pausing, walking slowly to allow myself to listen to my heart. As a child, I trusted my intuition implicitly, following it everywhere. As an adult, I felt anxious listening to my intuition because I had been taught not to. Yet, I was at peace because I felt that my heart had started to guide me. I wrote later that day:

As I step forward into the next phases of my life, it will be with purpose, with direction, and with heart. I know that there will be pain. I know that I will be challenged, as we all are on our true paths. I know that I will feel loss and sorrow, too. But more than anything, I will feel like me, and that is what matters. As I think on what I am called to do, on what my vocation may be, I must share that it is a mystery. That feeling of being scooped up, of being carried to a higher plane of existence is entirely misguided and misleading.

However one might speak of the feeling—whether as one's heart whispering to them, or as God speaking truth, or as a guiding force, or intuition—the feeling is undeniably gentle. This whisper can only be heard in the peaceful moments between actions, in the space allowed for it. This calling is omnipresent, and yet transparent, unseeable. It cannot be heard unless listened for and even still, is sometimes missed.

There is no singular calling for me, no one vocation or path, there is no one job or mission for my life. The callings are like the quiet caresses of the wind through the leaves on a peaceful day, helping to share the multiplicitous beauty of life, if only we listen.

This summer, this life, the love I have felt, and the losses I have endured... The pain that I have grown through, and the knots in my bark... The warmth of the sun and laughter of children... They all are present both in reality and in the shimmering fabrics of who I am. Every experience I have journeyed through, fought for, surrendered to, avoided, and passionately engaged with; they are all me. My life is eclectic, my fabrics are swirls of colors, glistening in the sun and sparkling in the moon. My life is illegible and unreadable, it is malleable, and yet grounded. It is frightening and seeks the unknown. It is exciting and foreboding, beckoning and full of pain, of love, of joy. I cannot say where my life will lead, but I can promise that it will be mine, lived fully as me.

As I reflect on the last few months of my life—each moment coalescing into who I am now, who I am becoming—I feel profound change on the horizon, unnamed until right now. I have felt anxious about my future, knowing the stability of my past, uncomfortable with the independence of freedom. I have been strung along through my life, mostly following the guidance of others, the call of society. There are so few things that I have felt authentically proud of, fulfilled by. Things that are amazing to others are dull and colorless to me.

So much of my life has been committed to the machinations of a construct unfathomably large, the hive mind of a sleeping humanity. It is nearly impossible to escape from the pervasive will of the many. It drowns out the gentle call of my heart.

Imagine for a second, if you will, that each person's energy is like a cup of water being filled. Everyone is different, certain activities might fill one person's cup while draining another. But every life is a cup. For the last many years, I have been living in a world where simply doing my daily tasks drains my cup. My environment has torn a hole in the bottom of my vessel and no matter how much I put into my cup, it floods out the bottom. I don't mean to be depressing or dismal, but I do want to be alarming. I have felt for years that there must be a better way to live life, and I have been searching for it.

In my search I have come across many truths and many ideas that could be true. One of the simplest ideas I have found and developed is the idea of one's inside happiness and one's environmental compatibility. Largely, happiness, fulfillment, and joy come from within. There are choices that we can all make to put gratitude before anger, courage before fear, and action before inaction. We can choose to be positive and optimistic in a world full of fear. This is an inside choice and some claim that by turning this dial, it will solve all problems. I do not believe this, though. I think that one's environmental compatibility is as important as one's inner journey.

To be fulfilled, a person absolutely must be living their life in a way that is fit for them. Every person is different, and it is nearly impossible to look to others for affirmation that an environment matches a person's vocational necessity. Each of us must walk our own path, paths even. Each of us must listen to the gentle callings of our hearts and align our actions and environment with those callings. Even if I choose all the right things on the inside, I still must escape the vacuum of inaction and stagnancy. To live in the world that I want and to align myself with the environments I want it is likely that I must create that world, manifest it.

My journey forward is set with the intention and the true north of this idea: For my life to be as it should be, I must listen to my heart and manifest the reality that I need. There is nothing stopping me but me. I do not know where I will be guided, I do not know which oceans I will cross first or which people I will come to love. I do not know what beautiful colors *will be added to the fabrics of my life. I only know that I must walk forward with the faith that if I listen to my heart, all else will fall into place. I know that I am here on this Earth to do something good, as we all are, and I intend to stride forward, courageously manifesting the world that I know can exist.*

My future is rife with opportunity, to love and to mourn, to grow and to learn. As I set forth, I will bring with me all the experiences that have made me who I am, I am draped in the fabrics of my past. I will choose to help not hurt, to strive instead of balk. I will give of myself the best that I can, always hoping that by being me, I can treat the afflictions of humanity and of our shared home. I will not name myself that which I am not. I am a healer and an artist, I am a visionary and a philosopher, I am a wanderer and I am a writer. I will never give up on myself or my life. I choose life in the face of death. I choose to be me.

I sign this Covenant of the Magnolia Tree to myself:
Faolan Sugarman-Lash

Looking back, I am shocked with the clarity and truth in my writing. Given the pain of my breakup, I'm shocked that I was able to tap into such a deeply powerful place. I wrote the words from my unconscious soul but quickly forgot them in the sadness of my current situation. My unconscious knew but my conscious had to play catch up yet again.

Abruptly, a month after my breakup and months after my Covenant, I reread it and knew it was time to do mushrooms again. Somehow every time I've wanted to do mushrooms, it's felt like a calling, like the little voice of the divine is telling me to do them. It's a subtle yet powerful feeling, just like the call I felt at the top of the tree. I never know what I'm going to get from the experiences, but they always come at the right time. Until it's time to do them again, I never want to. I never crave psychedelics the same way I do other drugs like weed and alcohol. Psychedelics, for me, are a once-in-a-while calling.

In January 2020, I ate mushrooms for the second time. As they kicked in, I started to sob. I felt the visceral reality of heartbreak strike me. The mushrooms led me straight to the heart of my grief and let me sit in it without turning away. For a time, I laid in bed and let my tears flow. Then, as the tears slowed and came to a stop, so too did my grief. I had gone to the depths of my sadness. While there, I was able to accept it and embody it. As I did, I was able to let it go. In a moment of inspiration, I wrote:

I feel whole as who I am. I thought that I wanted to figure out how to think about myself in relation to women, but I needed to think about myself in terms of myself. I am whole as who I am. That's the point.

Something clicked and I recognized in myself my own completeness. I saw that I truly didn't need another person. Where before, I had understood this logically, I didn't embody it. Now, I had a chance to feel that reality. I wasn't nearly done integrating the lesson with my sober self, but I experienced it viscerally on mushrooms and now knew it was possible. Mushrooms helped me let go of my fractured reliance on external validation and feel my wholeness for the first time.

As my tears subsided, my adventurous spirit returned. I played my favorite album, Coldplay's *Everyday Life*, and stood up. I put on my favorite clothes—a dark green T-shirt, shorts, and bare feet—and went to look out the window. It was a beautiful, sunny day in Santa Clara and all I wanted to do was go outside. So, I did.

I brought my housemate with me, and we walked around the neighborhoods. I looked at plants and saw beautiful, natural, alien shapes. I looked at Oranges growing on trees and was overcome with a sense of awe and gratitude at the simple reality that plants grow fruit for us to eat. (I saw an old stuffed bear that someone left sitting on the top of a wall. Mysterious.)

When we got home, I told my friend I was going on a solo adventure and thanked him for trip-sitting me. I set out with my backpack, my journal, my headphones, a water bottle, and my longboard. I skated away from my house, marveling at the beauty of life and maintaining my balance effortlessly and unconsciously. Like the first time I did mushrooms, all self-judgment was gone.

Then, I was at my bench. I looked at it the way someone would look at their child, parent, or favorite pet. That bench signified so much to me and would become the home for my inner revolution into peace, love, God, and beauty.

As I sat down, I looked around me, pulled out my journal, and wrote:

The Picturesque Moment

How to describe the wonder of the present moment? Words can't do justice to the profound awe I feel just to be alive, sitting here on this bench, blooming! I am growing. The future expands forward from me, sitting on this bench writing with number 2 pencils on a crisp, blue/white page. The page was so blank and beautiful. Now my words crawl across these lines, demanding space in the great big world. It is my right to be heard and to express myself. I can feel my energy so at peace with who I am and so grateful.

Then, it was as if I zoomed out of my body and saw myself as an old man, sitting on the very same bench. No, it was more than that, I became both the old version of me and the current version of me simultaneously. As that dual creature of two ages, all my potential paths unfolded between young and old and then became just two paths. The first path was one of conformity. The second path was one of authenticity.

In the first path, I was a businessman in a suit and tie. I had money and acclaim. I was stable. But it wasn't right. In the second path, I was a writer dressed in old clothes and with a sparkle in my eye.

I knew, with certainty, that the older version of me wanted to be a writer, not a businessman. I felt it in every bone of my body. I embodied my future self as if writing an autobiography and I didn't want to write a story about the version of me who gave up on his dreams and his heart. I wanted to write the story of Faolan flourishing, of Faolan the writer. It was so simple, as if every doubt I'd ever had was gone. I knew, in that moment, that I could only ever follow my authentic path. I knew that I had to write, to make art. I knew that I could never succumb to the path of conformity.

The next thing that happened was equally beautiful. I looked up at the branches of the Magnolia tree and for the first time, noticed the way that they splayed every which way, as if reaching for the sun in the pinball machine of nature. I was awed by the complexity of each branch. I pulled out my journal again and wrote:

The world from my eyes has value! I have so much love for everything. The way the sunshine touches the magnolia blossoms is so beautiful. Sometimes life feels like it's crooked and like it doesn't know where it's headed. But we are always heading towards the sun. The crookedness is like the branches of the magnolia tree, holding so much potential, being so much potential just as they are. How does nature do it? Life is so beautiful!

From the magnolia tree, I found beauty, peace, and acceptance for the crookedness of each path. Our paths, like the branches of the magnolia tree, aren't straight. They are crooked and complex, but ultimately, they are all reaching toward the sun. Each tree grows toward the sun in different shapes and sizes, just as each person's authenticity grows in a way unique to that person. We can learn much from trees.

When things seem to be going in the wrong direction, when you seem lost, remember that you are growing toward the sun with all your might, in your own way. Perhaps it is autumn and you are letting parts of you go. Perhaps it is winter and you are leafless, unable to feel the energy of the sun coursing through you. Enjoy these times, for they have much to offer and know that, in time, spring will come again and with it the beauty of life born anew and the scent of wisteria in the air.

At the end of my trip, I wrote:

Life is about writing our own story. It's not about just living. There's so much more agency allowed. It's about making it mine and being me, powerfully!! Open arms and grateful. Bright eyed.

Yet still, every realization, every victory demands a challenger. This one was no exception.

-18-

THE DRAGON IS WELCOMED

"Since shouts and taps, stones and sticks had failed to do the trick, there was only one thing left: drop the nuclear bomb called depression on me, not with the intent to kill but as a last-ditch effort to get me to turn and ask the simple question, "What do you want?" When I was finally able to make the turn— and start to absorb and act on the self-knowledge that then became available to me—I began to get well."

— PARKER J. PALMER

It was good that I came to know the crookedness of life, because right after my breakthrough came a breakdown. As you've seen my realizations are always tested and I've needed to practice them before embodying them. I knew I didn't need another person for my fulfillment and was shown that Truth again on shrooms, but still, when I was rejected by a woman I asked out, all my darkness returned, viciously, suddenly.

Like in a classic storybook, right before the hero finds their treasure, there is a final battle. For me, my final battle took place almost exactly one year after I wanted to step in front of a car to end my life. My final battle with my Dragon was a vicious affair stemming from insecurity, lack, and dreams of non-reality.

After taking shrooms and glimpsing my inner Truth, I was still too scared to act. My Depression Dragon saw this and took it as the perfect opportunity to jump on me. When my depression had come in the past, it was as if I were sinking into a sea of honey, slowly coming to terms with the fact that I was drowning and couldn't swim. In the past, I had been mildly aware of my downward spirals and had been able to watch them happen. This time, it was sudden, like a storm on a clear day.

Every time my depression came, it was triggered by my feelings of being unworthy of love. This time was no different. I asked out a woman and was rejected. The rejection catalyzed my inner unworthiness. It wasn't the rejection itself that brought my depression about, but what the rejection triggered in me. My lack of self-worth led me to inaction. I knew I needed to do something but didn't. Then my depression was there. When my lack of self-worth was exposed, everything else fell apart. Knowing that it might be its last chance, my Depression Dragon launched itself at me with all its might.

On February 17, 2020, I wrote:

It feels like the walls of life and the world are crumbling, crushing me from all directions. My heart is heavy, and my eyes are ripe with tears. On such a spectacularly beautiful day my insides are shriveling. My arms feel weak, and the edges of my mouth are weighted, making my smile increasingly crooked and false.

I hate this feeling. I'm deeply sad and I don't know why. Well, I have inklings.

I promised myself I would write and so I am but it's not really helping. I want to run away, to curl up in a ball and cry. I want to find the tallest rock in the middle of the sea and release a scream of ancestral magnitude. I want to shout and at the same time it feels like my vocal cords are coming apart, one at a time, and all at once, like a piano exploding as it plummets into the earth.

The birds are singing and the sun is shining, and yet inside I am crying. Am I simply attached to this depression or is this depression attached to me? They are very different conundrums entirely.

People make themselves so busy, filling their time with nothing and yet they are happy. I can't understand our society and I think it's killing me. I feel alone. No one understands.

This week has been hard because of my longing for romantic love, but it feels like it goes even deeper, beyond just a longing. It feels like this is the heart of my depression. The dragon is back to fight me once again. It's reaching for my legs, grasping, whispering sour somethings into my ear... telling me I am alone, that I am weak, that life is hopeless. It is bristling with false courage and is enlivened by my aching heart.

And yet all at once, I can feel it exposed, scattering under the light I shine on it. The monster is false, and it is ephemeral, released into the ether with a swift blow.

Then, suddenly, I am exhausted. Holding onto the light is so hard, it is so heavy. As I drop the lantern and the light winks out, it comes back, once again wrapping its dark tendrils around my heart, blocking out the love that exists around me.

I struggle with the monster, with the pain.

It is a hard and striking realization that even in wonderful weather depression can find its way into my life. To be moved from seasonal in terms of weather and months to seasonal in terms of the varying parts of life is dangerous. The monster has regained its element of surprise and now I must be wary constantly, maintaining vigilance even on the most wonderful days.

It's hard to explain what it's like to be depressed. It is such a personal thing. It's irrational.

There is so much life yet to be lived and yet it is all tainted with darkness. I don't know how to manage the turmoil and darkness inside. I guess I will just sit with it, learn from it, and be grateful for my demons, for it is my demons that will teach me the most.

When my depression saw my fear and unworthiness keep me from being my True Self, it gave me a great kick in the balls. For years, I thought of depression as the enemy, because it felt horrible. In this last battle with my beast, I learned to accept the darkness in the same way I accepted light, as part of reality. I listened to it. What I heard shocked me: It was trying to help.

My depression saw me find my Truth and wanted to help me keep it. I saw that it responded not to my Truth, **but to my fear of enacting my Truth**. It was trying to help me overcome my fear. It came when I was too afraid to be my full self, catalyzed by rejection and the soreness inside me from my traumas.

Every time I've been depressed, I've come out of depression with more wisdom and direction. When I was a sophomore, depression found me on the monkey bars and showed me that I needed to journey into the unknown. When I was a junior, depression found me in New Zealand and showed me that I needed to welcome my soul back. When I went back to Santa Clara, depression showed me that in order to want my life, I would have to live it authentically. This time, depression was showing me I needed to walk the talk and listen to my Truth.

Depression has been my greatest teacher in life. It has been there for me at my lowest lows, and it has helped me do the painful work of finding myself. It was not easy to be in and it did not feel good, but it was important every time. After all these years of hating spiritual depression because it felt awful, I accepted it as a part of the path and by doing so welcomed it into my life for good. Depression will never go away, but we can learn to experience it with gratitude, curiosity, and even wonder.

Depression is a teacher. How we receive its teaching is up to us. We can fight it and get detention, or we can listen and learn from it. We can tell it to shut up and refuse to do our homework or we can take notes, journal, and do the work. Depression is not a bad, shameful thing, but a teacher. What a gift!

There is a marvelous book called *Let Your Life Speak*, by Parker J Palmer. In his book, Palmer goes into his experiences with depression in order to explain that depression is not evil. He describes depression as our True Self's last resort to communicate to us something that we're ignoring. In that reframe, depression becomes an ally as opposed to a villain. So, while it felt like a Dragon, it's intention was to teach me something. Now, I can ride on the dragon instead of fighting it.

I interviewed over 30 people to prepare for this book. I asked them about depression, mental health, and authenticity. An amazing thing happened in one of my interviews. The interviewee and I concluded that depression is like an alarm. It comes with us wherever we go, hovering behind us, waiting until we're being particularly obstinate in our refusal of the Truth. Then, when our True Self has tried everything that it can to communicate gently with us and has failed, it uses the alarm.

The alarm is loud and ear splitting. It is trying to make us realize something. The longer we go without realizing that thing, the more the alarm will ring in our ears. It rings so loudly that it hurts. At first it's unbearable. But, for many of us, realizing what it's trying to show us is even more unbearable. So, we bear the pain and it transforms into suffering. Eventually, it's been ringing so long that we don't notice it except for a dull ache or fog.

When we pay attention to the ache and the fog, the alarm comes back in full force and makes us feel all the pain that we've been putting aside. Then, on the other side of the pain is the Truth that we've been avoiding so desperately. The reason that my depression came back this time was because I was drifting away from the Truth that I had learned. I had seen the beauty of my life while on mushrooms—I found my calling as a writer and as the narrator of my life—but was too scared to act, so depression came. It was pissed that I was going to let myself down again.

My True Self was having none of this and it went straight to alarms, full force blaring. It was incredibly painful for me, but it's what I needed. It was like jumping into an ice-cold pond in order to wake up to reality. I was losing touch with my heart again and my True Self was so pissed. After all the work I had done, I was going to let myself slide back into the doldrums of fantasies and delusion? No way.

So far, my depression has never had to go this far again. After this experience, I began to prioritize my intuition over everything else. I started to listen to my inner whisper and pay attention to what felt right for me. Paying attention doesn't always mean learning quickly. Sometimes depression still keeps me lying on the floor, but I don't push it away. By welcoming the pain, I speed up the healing process. By choosing to listen to what depression is teaching me, I merge with it, and it evaporates.

I like to imagine my True Self hovering above me. It can't speak to me in words, so it uses all different sorts of other things to get my attention. Maybe it sends me signals through tiny impulses of intuition. Maybe it uses my body to make me pay attention to my feelings. Maybe it only speaks to me when I'm silent and still. In the moments when I'm not listening, it's hovering over my head frustrated and amused at my ignorance. When I don't listen, it becomes a billowing darkness that covers my entire existence.

It's as if I'm navigating a maze and it's floating above. My True Self can see the way to the prize in the middle but can't communicate with me. I'm blind and completely lost, stumbling into walls and facing terrible monsters on the way. I'm preoccupied in my rush and anxiety to get to the goal. All I really need to do is stop and become aware of my higher self guiding me. I need to have faith that even in the unknown, even in the darkness of my personal ignorance, there is a part of me that knows where it's going. If I ignore my True Self, it has no choice but to use pain to wake me.

The kicker is this: People fear Truth. People are scared to believe that they matter. I can't think of any other reason that we so viciously ignore our pain and True Selves in favor of letting ourselves suffer the ringing of an incessant alarm bell. People fear the Truth of their own significance, because it means seeing the world in a completely new way. It means acknowledging that there is work to do, that we each have unique purposes to fulfill. It means letting go of our pasts, of people who no longer are right for us, of our old conceptions of reality, of our old selves. It means having the courage to stand up and believe in our convictions despite the doubt. It means having faith in our deepest Truths to guide us.

This was the gentle vanquishing of my Dragon. By learning to love and appreciate it for what it was, I started to listen. By loving the most painful part of myself, I was able to fully love my whole self and welcome my fullness into existence once more.

Over time, I've learned to avoid spiraling into depression by maintaining awareness of my intuition and by listening to my dragon's wisdom.

Constantly, as our inner voice calls to us, we must confront what is uncomfortable—what is in the unknown beyond our lived experience. In order to create and manifest our callings into the world, we must overcome our fears and have courage. When I didn't overcome these fears and instead escaped into non-realities—TV, looking to others for meaning, watching porn, drinking alcohol, etc.—my Truth had no means but to hit me over the head with a depression holding the weight of my dreams; heavy. Manifesting our true selves into the world is challenging work, but it is what is required of us.

This last bout with my Dragon set the stage for me to welcome all Truth into my life, no matter how painful. It freed me from hating depression and let me accept my Dragon as a friend. When depression comes now, I let it, and as I do, I learn from it, and it passes.

I welcomed my darkness and took another step to becoming whole, to finding my answer, but still, I didn't know "Why Live?"

An Intermission

THE BEGINNING AGAIN

The journey so far has been tumultuous and winding. I cleared the slate and lifted my fog. I stopped suffering (mostly) and accepted my pain (mostly). I did a lot of work. Yet, despite everything, compared to the magnitude of my following experiences, it was like a lake to an ocean.

The rest of my story departs from the world of certainty and ventures into the spiritual realms of mysticism and beauty. My healing journey was important, and it mattered, but only because it set the stage for me to experience the fullness of life's gifts. The rest of my journey leaves the realm of certainty and ventures into the spiritual realm, where things are known without being explainable, where meaning is intrinsic without being claimed or understood, and where Gods and the Divine permeate everything.

The journey so far has been simple, though convoluted. I feel fairly confident that I have described my experiences adequately up to this point. From here forward,

I am equally confident that my words cannot do justice to my experiences.

Writing about what cannot be described was like trying to hold the entirety of the ocean in my hands. I could understand the task, in theory, but its magnitude was beyond comprehension.

As you read, forgive my inadequacy and the insufficient nature of language. Keep an open mind and soul. Let your heart discern what is True, not the judging of your consciousness. Feel into my words and find the ones that resonate within you.

Welcome to Part 6, the spiritual payout.

PART 6
FINDING YOUR GOD

ALIVE

"

*And he to whom worshiping is a window, to open but also
to shut, has not yet visited the house of his soul whose windows are from dawn to dawn.*

"

— KHALIL GIBRAN

-19-

BREATHE IN STILLNESS

"Whenever there is stillness there is the still small voice, God's speaking from the whirlwind, nature's old song, and dance..."
– ANNIE DILLARD

Take a deep breath. In through the nose and out through the mouth. Sit up straight. Feel the ground beneath you. Be here. Breathe deeply again. Close your eyes and pause in presence for a moment. Be aware. Take your time and come back when you're ready.

Breathing is the most natural thing in the world. Our breath is with us at all moments of our lives. Our breath continues while we sleep, while we run, while we play, while we work. Our breath is here, always. It is a foundation to find stillness, to find presence.
In the spring of 2020, the world spiraled into chaos when Covid-19 descended. Breath was taken away by a plague.

With Covid-19 came upheaval. Normal, daily life was disrupted, and a new reality became normal. For the world at large, Covid-19 was a painful experience—countless people died, anxiety rose globally. A cloud of the unknown descended in waves and with the unknown came opportunity and with opportunity came fear.

In the spring of 2020, America spiraled into chaos when George Floyd was murdered. Breath was taken from a human by another human.

Fear transformed into pain and pain into purpose. On May 26th, despite the virus, thousands of people took to the streets fighting for every human's right to breathe, and especially for those who have had it unjustly taken away.

The great sadness of death touched me, and my heart broke for the families who lost loved ones to the plague of Covid and to the plague of racism. It was a powerful time to be alive, to bear witness to the grand unfolding of Life.

In a paradoxical way, the turmoil, stress, and pain of life around me juxtaposed my personal journey. The pain and suffering around me was dark and visceral whereas my transient experience of life was slow and peaceful. Many people were trapped in the solitude of their homes with only their unresolved traumas and the horrific news for company whereas I had moved through much of my own trauma and stayed distanced from the news. Hatred, fear, and tension were ubiquitous.

It's hard to describe how it was to watch everything happen from my newfound place of equanimity and distance. When I welcomed my depression dragon into me and it transformed into the voice of my true self, I lost my capacity to hate. Instead of letting anxiety and fear pull me around, I chose to spend my time becoming present to the beauty beneath the pain and to the essence of pain itself. We always have the choice to engage with the hate and respond to it or to hold space for its existence but not engage. Many of us don't know we have this choice.

Our world is conditioned to experience constant forced emotion. 24-hour news and the mass media industries sell us stories about the world, about ourselves, and about anything at all. It is a money-making industry. In the spring of 2020, I stopped listening to any of it in order to hear the Truth inside me and in the buzzing of the bees and the touch of the breeze.

I spent the better part of my spring becoming aware of the beauty around me. Amid the tumult and anxiety, I found stillness and peace and recognized it even more clearly.

Some part of me felt guilty about my privilege, about the color of my skin, about my health. Some part of me let that guilt lead to feelings of unworthiness and to shame. But, at the end of the day I knew I was on my own path and that nothing could be more important. Without my experience in Ghana, I would have felt much worse. I would have felt like I needed to act, to do something to help. But, because I had learned to forgive myself for not being able to solve all the world's problems, I was able to focus on my own personal path and know that my work mattered, or would matter eventually.

That being said, it wasn't easy for me to watch people suffer, to watch as my black and brown brothers and sisters died at the hands of people who looked more like me. It was deeply painful and I felt it fully. I let the pain of the injustices wash over me and I let my tears fall. No one should be ostracized from the greater community of humans. We are all the same creatures, the same team.

I struggled to watch people suffer but chose to have faith in my work over all else because, ultimately, I knew that the work I was doing was to heal people and with healing would come less violence, more compassion, empathy, and love. I stuck to my own path and trusted that by doing so I would have a greater impact than letting myself be drawn into anything but my work. I was tearing down systems of oppression in my own way.

On March 13, Santa Clara shut down all in-person living situations and classes. 80% of the student body went home. I decided to stay. I was paying for rent. I loved my house. I loved the sunshine and the warmth of California. So, when most people left, I stayed. I spoke with my parents and my friends about my decision. Many people thought that I was making a bad decision and that I would be safer at home. But, like all my best decisions, I followed my intuition and not the "prevailing wisdom" AKA fear/bullshit/who knows.

Each morning, I woke up before everyone else, in the darkness of night, got dressed, gathered my books, my backpack, and journals, and crept down the stairs to brew a cup of chai. Then, I slowly and quietly left my house through the front door. I stepped outside into the cool, morning air that greeted me and woke my senses to life.

I walked, taking in the sounds of morning birds, the smell of wet mist and sights of pre-dawn. The stars still shone gently in the morning light. As I walked, I slowed my breathing and my step, carefully balancing my mug so as to not spill any tea.

There's a part of *The Alchemist*[4] that I never understood until carrying my tea in the beauty of dawn. In the book, there is a story about a boy who traveled far away to seek the secret of happiness from a wise man in his castle. In the castle, there were many wonderful things, scrolls and paintings and other pieces of art. The boy went to the wise man inside the building and asked for help with his quest. The wise man offered him a spoon with drops of oil in it and told the boy to go see the beautiful things in the palace, but to not drop the oil. The boy returned with the oil but missed all the beauty. The wise man tells him to try again. He goes back out and sees the beauty but returns with no oil. The wise man says this: "The secret of happiness is to see all the marvels of the world, and never forget the drops of oil on the spoon."

As I walked in the mornings with my tea, observing the wonder around me, listening to the calls of mourning doves, and smelling the coming sun, I had to also balance my hand and maintain awareness of my tea. Day after day it went like that until I connected my experience to the

[4]By Paolo Coelho

story in the book. I realized that true joy is being aware of the wonder and beauty that constantly surrounds us while also maintaining awareness of our purpose. The challenge is to carry our unique purpose forward while feeling the majesty of life and to intertwine the two.

When I arrived at the bench, I set my tea down and set up my meditation timer. I closed my eyes and followed my breath. The art of mindfulness meditation is challenging and also simple. I noticed my breath coming in and going out of my body, feeling each sensation of the air on my nostrils and the rising and falling of my chest and stomach. As thoughts inevitably came up, I tried to watch them without engaging and with full compassion for myself.

Each morning, as the sun rose, I sat in darkness awaiting light, eyes closed, in awareness of my own thoughts coming and going. The key is not to force a clear, blank mind, but to allow whatever is happening to happen and gently return to awareness of the breath. Mindfulness meditation is not about force or judgement or becoming a superior person. It's about developing awareness and compassion and presence. The most important part about this form of meditation is being present with what is without judgment and with love.

Eventually I slowly opened my eyes, stretching each finger and toe, wiggling my body and smiling at the newly arrived sunshine. I journaled about my gratitudes, then my work began: Studying presence.

In a most tumultuous time, I settled into my purpose and breath, in order to find meaning and peace. Humanity has always experienced suffering and likely will for years to come. In a suffering world, know that in stillness and awareness you may always find peace, and in peace you may let the Flow find you.

-20-

THE FLOW OF LIFE AND DEATH

*"Death is no enemy, but the foundation of
gratitude, sympathy, and art."*
– ANITA DIAMANT

Let me speak now of life and death, birth and leaving, the continuous flow of presence. As each moment is born, so does it die. I saw this first on mushrooms. As each person is born, so too will they die. As each second passes, new babies are born, and new people die. Every moment, birth, life, and death are certain. It is constant. It is cyclical. It is beautiful, tragic, and moving.

So many times in the spring of 2020, I leaned back and watched Wind blow the leaves in the trees above me. I closed my eyes and listened to the sounds of life. Even in stillness, everything was in the Flow. Life is always flowing around us, waiting to be noticed, waiting for us to slow down enough to see it and appreciate it, to wake up to its magnificence, and root ourselves in it.

As I sat at my bench, reading about existence, non-existence, compassion, detachment, equanimity, and peace, the beauty of Life began to speak to me. As I opened into my role as part of the grander flow of Life and death, I started to hear whispers of something. It was whispering wordless meanings, as if placing Truths into my brain that were beyond my full comprehension. I settled deeper into myself and my lack of self, into the Flow of All.

In the Flow, I began to understand where it was taking me, and I opened up to it. I watched as the Flow brought all life to death, as it compassionately and unbiasedly brought each being into non-being. I watched as it brought Life into existence and transformed one life into another.

I watched the squirrels run around trees chasing each other. I watched them dig into the earth to bury their food. I watched the especially brave ones come closer to my bench, sneak under my legs, and around my feet. I watched hummingbirds flit from flower to flower, pausing in midair, wings beating at a furious pace. I watched each day as my magnolia tree's bare branches turned into buds, then flowers and small fuzzy leaves, and finally birthed a full assortment of deep green foliage. I watched as the wind blew and died, coming and gone. Each moment, each animal, each plant held such wonder, such divine peace.

I too watched people wander through the gardens. Many were parents with young children on scooters or bikes. I watched the kids laugh and run or pause to inspect an interesting patch of dirt. I watched as elders found their way more slowly into the peace of the gardens, appreciating each purple, red, and orange rose. I watched old couples hold hands, hobbling gently past me, content to be at peace in their own time. I watched people of all ages and races, of all shapes and sizes flow through the garden.

Each moment came and then died. I watched the flow. I was present to Life and death, to impermanence. In watching Life come and go, birth and fade, tears came to my eyes and laughter bubbled from my stomach. I felt deep joy, gratitude, and grief. Each being that flowed past was part of the greater flow of Life and yet each being held its own space, foraged for its own food, played its own games, smiled its own smile, sang its own tune, and beat its own heart. In each simple beating heart, whether the rapid hummingbird's or slow old woman's, lay a beauty, the beauty of Life.

Life. Life is so beautiful. It is all around us, always around us, in us, just waiting to be appreciated, to be loved. As Life exists, it yearns to be lived fully, to be lived with intention and gratitude. It demands that you recognize its finite nature, its fleeting reality. From the Truth of death, it shows you purpose and peace. Death can gift you meaning simpler and more expansive than any other.

As Life comes, it goes. For all beings, each life is in a perpetual dance with death. As Life is born, all lives die, and yet Life never dies. The flow of Life experiences constant birth, being, and death. But it is in the manner of the individual, not the greater flow, that inevitable death brings meaning and peace to each of us.

For many years, I had been in my own dance with death, with meaning, and with Life. As I suffered in my lack of self, as I kept my pain covered beneath layers of shame, I became intimate with a sort of non-living. I experienced a slow dying process, letting each day slip through my fingers, like fine sand on a beach. My heart was closed, and my life was dark.

In the gardens, as I witnessed the flow of Life and death, I started to dance with more vigor. I shook off my morbidity and my slow death and learned to face mortality head on as a member of Life. As I watched the life around me inevitably lead to death, the flow of my own life and death became enmeshed with the greater flow of all Life and death, cleansing me of any desire to escape my life, to die before my time. By watching without judgement, I learned to appreciate each life and its inevitable end. I learned to appreciate my life and to welcome the certainty of my death, like an old friend come to remind me of my Life's treasures. No more would I seek to die, but would instead walk next to Death, letting him guide me and show me a more full life than I had ever sought before.

Once, a young client came to me and shared that she didn't think she would live many more years. She shared that she had always believed she would die in her 20s. As I listened, I heard a deeper truth under her words, one that I was intimately familiar with. What she was saying was, "I don't want to live very much longer." I asked her to explain more, and she shared that her life had always been painful, that she didn't want to get old or experience her body losing its youth. She was explaining her relationship to death.

We all have relationships with death, in general, and with our own. Many of us prefer to not address the relationship, to leave it in the darkness of our being, cast into shadow by the daily tasks we pursue. Many people are afraid of death, whether their own, that of a loved one, or in general. With this fear of death comes a fear of living fully. With the fear of death comes a fear of Life because Life is death. With the fear of death comes a fear of a Life. I say it three times. With the fear of death, comes a fear of Life. Pay attention! There is no way to live without death.

For millennia, immortality has been the human treasure, sought by so many. In society today, we seek to immortalize ourselves into computers so our brains may live on beyond the years of our bodies. We seek to escape death. But it cannot be done. With Life comes death. All that lives must die eventually. And yet, the beauty of death is that with death, comes Life. With a full acceptance of death comes the ability to live each moment in awareness of its fleeting nature. With death, each life opens into a beautiful, spectacular array of brilliance, each moment bursting like fireworks in the sky only to fade away, dying and leaving behind space for a new burst of light to be born. Each burst demands our participation.

The flow is constant, ever-present, surrounding us. The flow is beautiful, whole, rich. The flow is all we have. As I accepted my own death, I was struck by grief. With a full acceptance of my own mortality came tears. But more than tears, were the smiles and more than the smiles was the brightness of my eyes and of life around me. A moment of divine serendipity brought me into contact with the fullness of death and through it, Life.

I was home in New England, in the mountains. I set off in the late afternoon heat with my backpack on my shoulders and my friend, Owen, in tow. We wandered through fields of grasses and small bushes into the forest. The summer forests of New England are wild, serene, full of life, and smell of the best kind of dirt. As we pushed our way up the mountain side, we laughed in companionship and moved through deeper topics. We breathed hard and kept a steady pace.

At the top of the mountain, we stopped and looked out on the rolling hills of the Berkshires extending into the distance. We found a patch of tall grasses near a slate stone to sit on and enjoy our afternoon snack. We watched paragliders swoop and dive and float in the distance and smiled in the hot sun.

Then, Owen left me to camp on the mountain alone as I had requested. I had decided to give myself space to lean into death, into my life, and into the essence of my being. I pushed through some bushes and found a secret clearing on the other side of the summit. It was about 10 feet of flat earth covered in soft grasses. On one side of the clearing were small, wild blueberry bushes. On the other side was a steeply descending hill and beyond that was a majestic view of valleys, rolling hills, and farmland; humanity and nature interspersed.

I spread my tarp and laid back feeling the summer sun burning my skin. I covered my face with an extra t-shirt and promptly fell asleep. As I woke up, I felt the contentment that only comes from a timeless rest in nature. I had nothing to do and nothing to not do. I was simply able to drift into and out of sleep, always in the flow of Life and outside the realm of human time. I woke up feeling rested and took out my book.

I was reading a book called *The Five Invitations*[5]. It took me over a year to read despite being relatively short because of its depth. Each page spoke of death. Each story was centered around death. The full title is: *The Five Invitations - Discovering What Death Can Teach Us About Living Fully*. I opened the book to read the final chapter.

As I read each page in the beautiful book, I found myself more and more inside the flow. Distractions faded away and I was engrossed. I was inside the book, inside the stories, inside death and inside Life. As I read, Death and Life merged into one essence. Inside me, I felt Death and Life, grief and exuberance, ends and beginnings, here and gone. As I turned the last page of the book, I began to sob.

I looked out over the beautiful view: The sun crested the mountains, casting a golden, sunset glow on the hills and the clouds above. Tears fell from my eyes like heavy raindrops. As I cried, I found my heart breaking open and, once again, suddenly my tears turned into laughter. I

[5] By Frank Ostaseski

oscillated between tears and laughter, between heartbreak and gratitude, between grief and joy. Inside of my acceptance of death came a beautiful gratitude for Life. As my tears subsided, I wrote:

I will die. I must
But, dear God, I am
Grateful, bursting
With laughter and tears
To be given this gift
Of Life.

I am learning the meaning of stillness, surrender, aware-ness, awakening, peace, emptiness, God. That which is there but cannot be named, that can be experienced and felt but not explained. I'm realizing that in the pauses and the surren-der come the communion with ____, and sacredness, and the great interconnection.

Pausing is not about discovery of the profound or even growth of the self, but of stepping back from the experience of "me" to connect with "All" or "One." In that "All," there is no need to change or grow because it is a given that this will happen. It allows us to see the Truth, the Majesty, the Eternity. I will practice this inner stillness, in order to connect myself to what is real and True.

Inside Truth, love, presence, all-ness, and emptiness, there is no separateness, only ____. From this place, the unknown is known, Death is Life, and now is always. From this place, all is well, and thus always will be. From this place, can bloom the life I am meant to live. In the soil of ____, I will plant my roots. Once rooted, I will always pull my nutrients from the rich Earth, as I reach into the sky, seeking the essence of why I am here.

After writing, I paused. I took my headphones out and stopped the classical music in my ears. I laid down on my sleeping pad. I closed my eyes and followed my breath. I felt into death and into Life, into emptiness and fullness, into the existence of All and One. I laid there for an indeterminable time. Then, I heard something. Well, I didn't hear it, but my primal, animal instincts did. Without thinking, I stood up deliberately and slowly, backed to the edge of the cliffside and stood on a rock, facing my tarp and sleeping pad.

It was an unfamiliar sound of something grating against wood, leaves, and grass. Even as my rational brain sluggishly caught up to my instincts, I knew what it was. It was too consistent to be a mammal and too loud to be a bird. It was a snake. I knew it so certainly that I watched the bushes with eyes like a hawk, waiting for movement. Then, a bush moved, and another moved a few feet away. It wasn't just a snake but a great big rattlesnake. The bushes moved and swayed as it slithered through the undergrowth.

Through a break in the leaves, I saw it: at least three inches wide. I saw one part of it and then another part through a different break in the leaves. I felt my body slow down, watching, in total awareness. All thoughts vanished and I watched this living incarnation of death wind its way gracefully just inches from where my head had been seconds earlier. Then, I saw the end come into view, a magical gift of evolution, the rattle. It was silent, not making any noise as it slid through the bushes and finally away from my campsite. I hadn't scared it. I waited until I couldn't see or hear it anymore before my brain burst into a frantic chattering.

My brain said, rather all at once: "Faolan, that snake was Death come to greet you. Faolan, you could have died. Faolan, had you not taken your headphones out, you would likely be dead. Faolan, the snake brought you the gift of death and rebirth. Faolan, get out of here right now, I'm not ready to die." So, in a flurry of controlled activity, I packed all my gear up and made my way through the very bushes the snake had been in back to the trail. I walked down, my head in a blur. I witnessed Death in the form of a rattlesnake. I had been allowed to see my own mortality incarnate.

Looking back, the timing is simply incredible, almost beyond coincidence. For me to finish reading a book about death and life, about birth and rebirth; For me to come to terms with my own mortality and find true and profound gratitude for Life; For me to plant my life in the fertile soil of Death and then to witness Rattlesnake. It was undeniably a blessing I will never forget. It was as if nature was saying to me, "Faolan, welcome to the flow of Life. Here is a sign of your rebirth from dying into living, from death into life. Thank you for your gratitude for being alive and for holding death so compassionately." It was a moment of peace and of divine intervention that happens only in stories, except it happened to me.

Since that day, I have carried my mortality with me, letting it remind me to live fully, to hold myself accountable to what feels right, to be in the presence of flow. In the spring, I witnessed the flow of life and death. In the summer I was welcomed into the Flow as a willing member of the ride we all take from birth, through being, and into the realm beyond. In the Flow, I found a new way of life, a new power to draw on. With my acceptance of death came a gumption to live each moment with as much fullness as I could muster. With my acceptance of death, came the opportunity to shed my old skin and begin life anew, reborn with the intense passion of someone who knows he will die but who wants to live anyway. Despite the pain of loss and death, we must accept that it comes to pass, for only when we do will we shed our old skins and come alive.

When I saw my mortality, I found my Life. I put down roots into the nurturing soil of Nature and discovered my God.

-21-

GOD

"Those who wish to learn magic ought to begin by looking around them. All that God wished to reveal to man he placed right in front of him, the so-called tradition of the sun."-
– ANITA DIAMANT

I had many different religious influences in my life. My dad's family is Jewish. My dad's mom converted from Christianity to Judaism to marry my grandpa. My mom's family grew up with a western take on Hinduism and Yogism. My stepdad is a Sufi who leads Dances of Universal Peace of all over the world. I went to a Jesuit university where my best friends grew up Catholic and Christian. On top of that, I read about Buddhism whenever I could. My background let me have an open mind about spirituality and come to my own decisions about what my God is.

On my journey, I came to define my own God. God, for me, is just a placeholder word to name the human conception of the majesty of Life. Some substitute words for God are: Love, Connection, Buddha, Peace, The Universe, Reality, Truth, Spirit, Dharma, Allah, Earth, Nature, etc. None of these words do justice to the feeling I get when I'm truly awed and inspired by the simplest things. The feeling I got when I looked up at the pink flowers in my magnolia tree and saw the warm California sun shining through them is, to me, God.

God isn't a person or an entity, but a feeling. God is not some personified deity in the sky, but a recognition of a river of interconnectedness—the divine energy of creation that flows—of Life. It's profoundly simple and yet eternally impossible to explain. God simply Is without being described. God cannot be contained or understood, but it can be felt.

Metaphor does okay: God is the sun shining or the sound of rain. God is the laughter of a child and the smell of hyacinths. God is the tears that are shed when we acknowledge our mortality. God is the snake as it sheds its skin and God is all of us. God is the connecting energy of life and is Life itself. God is the path we walk to be who we truly are.

My spiritual journey meant coming to my own conclusions about God and Reality. I never felt bad about creating my own definitions and my path. I found true joy in defining God and spirituality for myself. Why should someone else define the things that are most important to me, that I base my life on? That being said, my definitions of God and spirituality are working definitions (or lacks of definitions). I don't expect to have come to the exact right conclusions at 23 and even if I have, I don't think that I could do those conclusions justice with words. God isn't a word, it's a feeling and you must, must, must find your own experience of it.

I fell into the river of Gods and the Divine rather unexpectedly, but right on schedule. Since going to Ghana, I had been reading books about God, about the Divine, and about Interconnectedness. Some books were fictional representations of how different authors see God. Some were non-fiction books literally describing different perspectives. At the end of the day, the walls around my rejection of God fell away and I found myself curious. For my whole life, I considered myself an atheist, but after years of healing and reading and living, I felt ready to not be. It was a slow building of energy that burst out when I wasn't expecting it. My God took me by surprise.

Inside each of us is an essence of the Divine. We are all connected to something bigger; something beyond our rational conception. That connection is always there waiting to be noticed but finding it can be the hardest journey of all. First you must believe that there is something, anything, indescribable, then you must believe that you are a part of that indescribable thing and that its grand majesty is beyond your words and yet known by your soul. The Truth is that you are no different than it because as it is All, you are in the midst of All. However, you must tap into it. Until you do, you're floating on the water in a boat of traumas and stories. Once you tap in, you become the water itself.

My boat had been falling apart over the last months, keeping me separate from the water with only shreds of leftover threads. As I worked to heal myself, I slowly took my boat apart without knowing what I was doing. Board by board, pain by pain, I demolished my boat until I floated down the river on just a few planks. Then, in a sudden flourish, they disappeared, and I fell into the river, never to return to any boat. Once I was in the river—and more so, of the river—I could never go back.

Imagine my psychedelic experiences as being dunked in the river of God. You feel it rushing past you, you revel in it, and then you are yanked out. With enough sober practice, you can ease yourself into that river every day of your life. Psychedelics gave me the opportunity to see Life differently, to feel different in my life. Each of my first three experiences opened doors to a greater understanding of my reality and of Reality itself. My first two experiences helped me find my physical presence and my Truest dream. My third experience showed me Divinity.

During my third trip, I was at a friend's house in her backyard. Flowers were in full bloom all around us and trees were bearing fruits. I picked up a vibrant, red flower in my hand, holding it without breaking it from its stalk. As I looked at the flower, I felt that all of Life was contained within it. More deeply, I recognized the flower as part of Nature, an embodiment of Earth and Life. That flower represented everything. That flower was the Divine source of all goodness, Nature incarnate. As I recognized the Divine source, I lifted my hand in exclamation and when I did, a moth landed on my outstretched finger and with it, a vision came to me.

In my vision, behind closed eyes, there was a massive, glowing, sphere-like flower atop a huge, leafy stalk. The plant was rooted in the Earth, which represented all of Nature, Energy, and Life. The plant itself represented humanity. The sphere-flower represented all human creation. It contained The Beatles and the atomic bomb. The plant carried the energy from the Earth into the sphere-flower.

I realized in that vision that humans are here to connect with Nature/Earth/Life in order to draw energy from the Divine source and collectively grow our sphere-flower... To create Godliness, which is a human embodiment of Life. God is not Life/Nature/Earth, but our human capacity to understand and recreate those Divine, all-encompassing, sources. God is our human conception of Life incarnate, and we are here to embody Godliness by sourcing our Energy, Truth, and Movement from the Divine Source of all things: Life.

However, often, what we create falls short of this aspiration because we are tainting the flow of Life with our trauma and shadow. Much of human creation isn't as profoundly wonderful as Nature is. The tainted flower isn't a perfect representation of the Earth. We must learn to channel the energy of Life and make it Godly, not hateful. Life must grow from a place of Truth and Healing.

Here's utopia: Every person—and thus the whole Divine plant—has healed from their individual and collective trauma and is connected directly to God and to Nature. When we're connected with the Earth, we connect with a higher power, and from that higher power, we are able to manifest true Beauty into the world, creating the right kind of "sphere-flower." Essentially, people who are rooted in Nature/Earth should create and those who are not, should find their personal Gods by rooting themselves in Life. So, how does one plant their roots in Nature and source their actions from their unique God?

This is the healing journey, and this is the spiritual journey; this is the path to love life. It is the search for our own unique Gods. Each person's "God" is unique and different depending on that person's experience. To heal is to find one's Spirit, which is to find the Spirit beyond; they are the same thing after all. Healing is, by definition, spiritual. When one heals, they connect to their personal God and become incarnations of Divine Truth and Life itself. As we heal, we must learn to walk our unique, spiritual paths.

If Life is the Earth that Humanity's plant is growing from, then the Sphere-Flower is our created representation of Life, named God. Life is Divine potential and pure good. Only when we are authentic—when we are channeling the Divine—do we create something that can be an addition to and not a distraction from what already is here.

From our connection to Divine energy and to our personal Gods, we manifest that energy which is beyond us, through us, and into the world. We are conduits. When we create from any place but Divine authenticity, we are not connected to our Gods, and we are creating distractions and muck that take away from the Divine Beauty of what is.

This is why healing trauma and becoming conduits for Life is important. When we are suffering and denying our own pain, our creations bring more trauma and suffering. When we heal and become Divinely authentic, our creations heal and bring beauty from Life to Life. Only after rooting ourselves in the Earth shall we find our personal Gods and only with our personal Gods shall we create that which Life intends of us.

An Intermission

ALL IS ONE
AND ONE IS ALL

Remember the metaphor: "When the messiah comes and you hold a sapling in your hands, first plant the sapling and then go to greet the messiah." This is the work after the work. As you heal your pain it's transformed into clay, with which you might craft a living, growing sapling. Your healed pain becomes your gift to offer the world and you shape it with your Artform. Only after offering your gifts to Life may you go to greet the messiah, or in other words, die peacefully.

Without offering your gift, there is no point in the rest of the journey of life and we all have gifts. Again. Without offering *Your Gift*, there is no point to the rest of the journey. Hear me.

After healing, after doing the hardest thing in my life, after forgiving myself, letting go of my trauma, accepting Death, and finding my God, my real journey began. You might think that this would be the end of it, that now I could settle down with a nice day job and three cats and enjoy myself... But, in nourishing my authenticity, came an even greater calling. From the silence and peace of being myself, I saw the next step: Create.

Remember the chapter, "Hurt People, Hurt People"? Well, the opposite is true, as well. People who heal themselves, help others heal and heal our collective.

The Earth does not need us to heal it. It needs us to heal ourselves so that we stop hurting it. The Earth is not a character with feelings and agency. The Earth responds to us and to how we are. When we suffer, the Earth suffers. When we heal, the Earth heals. In the world today, humans are suffering because we avoid Truth and the pain that comes with it, and thus, the Earth is, too.

This is the world we live in. This is the world we are lucky enough to share presence with. This Earth is always holding us, literally keeping us tethered to it so we don't float off into space. The Earth feeds us, shows us beauty, gives us limitless generosity. Even in the struggles and pain of living we may find the wonder of being alive, of being part of All. It is our duty to ourselves, to others, and to the world to heal and to offer our gifts. It is not about you or me, it is about Us. Not a simple "us," but Us.

"Us" as in God, as in All, as in Divine interconnection. Only by loving Life, can we Live. Only by becoming one with Life can we move Life in the right direction.

There are many monks who have devoted their lives to finding enlightenment, this obscure objective. They sleep

in caves and spend their time in meditation with the Oneness of All. I don't believe these monks have it right. Enlightenment is not an individual goal but the objective of
all Life. Enlightenment is not individually becoming One
with what is, but bringing All together into One. In order
to do this, you and I must heal, and from our healing bring
together All into One and each One into All. This happens
through creation, through Art.

Why Live? You may be feeling your answer already, but
we're not quite done. In addition to everything so far, you
must offer *your gifts*.

Part 7 is a slide. You've reached the pinnacle and you've
seen the views. Let Part 7 carry you back down the mountain and into your own life. Take it easy and enjoy the ride.

PART 7
A CALL,
A REVOLUTION,
AND A LETTER

ART

"

*Writing is the Excavator through the mountain
of darkness to find the Light.
Like a seed toward Sun, I write my own way out of the dark.
Of the Earth, toward the Sun, ever connecting both.
The work of Life.*

"

— ME

-22-

CALLING YOUR ART

*Playing the flute does not depend solely on practice
in the flute. I now play better than in the past
because I have found my true self. You cannot
reach lofty heights in art if you do not first discover
the unsurpassable beauty in your own heart. If you
would like to play the flute truly well, you must
find your true self on the path of awakening.*

– THE BUDDHA
THICH NHAT HANH

Capital "L" Life is the ever growing and expanding force that spreads through the desolation of space, creating, destroying, trying, dying, living, and being. We are part of Life and thus our purpose is, ultimately, the same. We are here to grow. Trees very naturally grow toward the Sun when rooted in the nourishing soil of Earth. Where are we to grow? What is the Sun to humans? What was my Sun? This is the question I still needed to answer to find my bigger answer. I had walked down my spiritual path to the point of naming my God, welcoming my mortality, and my depression, but still wasn't satisfied. Thus began the journey of finding my Art, discovering my callings, and creating my gifts. Who would have guessed that more trial and error awaited me?

In November of 2019, I did a vocational discernment assignment for a class. For the assignment, we answered three questions and then wrote short essays on three different career paths. The questions were: "What brings me joy?", "What am I good at?", and "What does the world need from me?". These questions brought me to three potential paths: Writer, coach, and entrepreneur. The word vocation comes from the words "to call" in Latin. This set the stage for me to find my callings.

In the summer of 2020, I graduated from college full of enthusiasm and Lifeforce into a global pandemic and an economic recession. I did it gladly because with graduation came the space to pursue my truth full time. In my Magnolia Tree Covenant, I made a commitment to, above all else, pursue my authentic path, no matter the cost.
I still didn't know Why I was alive but I sure as hell knew I was going to Live my life fully. That said, I didn't dive headfirst into being a homeless entrepreneur. That would come later. First, I played it safe.

In May, two important things happened. The first is that I accepted a backup job offer that would start in January of 2021. This gave me six months to figure out how to create something aligned with my journey. The second thing was that I coached my first practice client and loved it, but I got caught up in the movement of graduating from college, so my coaching hit the backburner.

After graduation, I moved home to New England. I got there on July 3rd, 2020. I started a part time job at my local bakery/pizza place on the 14th but only made it a week and a half before quitting. I liked the people, the atmosphere, and the free food but it just wasn't my path. I felt in my bones that I had more important things to be doing, so I quit on the 25th.

On the 20th, after another coaching conversation with a friend, I announced the launch of my life coaching practice. On the 22nd, I coached my first official client. On August 1st, I met Rattlesnake and accepted Death. On August 3rd, I hired my own coach for 800 out of the 900 dollars in my bank account. Two days later I signed my first client for 400 dollars a month.

In a month, I graduated from college, moved across the country, got a job, quit a job, started a business, accepted my mortality, hired a coach, and raised my hourly income from 13 dollars to 100. After years of healing, things clicked into place quickly.

I share this story not to brag, but to show that when you do your inner work, follow your intuition, and have courage in the face of your fears, your outside reality can change quickly for the better. I never expected to make 100 dollars an hour at age 22, less than two months after graduating from college, doing something I loved. It was energizing beyond belief.

One evening, I was completely exhausted from covering someone's shift at the bakery and totally forgot that I had a coaching call with my first client. She sent me a message and I ran frantically upstairs to call her. At that moment, there was nothing I wanted less than to work more, but I had made a commitment to her and to myself, so I did. As we talked, I felt my energy coming back, enthusiasm rushed into me. By the time I hung up, Life filled me to the brim. It was incredible.

Trust me when I say that you'll know when you find your gifts. It's not always easy to get started but once you do, the giving of the gift fills you up with the very energy of Life. Giving your gift connects you to your source. It's unlike anything else. The crucial piece is that you are giving something away (or charging), but not doing it for yourself. Parts 1-6 are all self-centered, crucially selfish. Part 7, Art, is all about offering yourself, manifesting your essence, in service of something bigger than yourself. This is the cash out of the whole damn spiritual thing and it's as simple as starting.

I used to ask successful entrepreneurs, artists, and travelers how they started. It was an enigma to me. I never understood how I could achieve what they had, how I could start a business or create something so big. It wasn't until I went through my spiritual awakening and found myself in Awe of Life that I realized my own capacity to create Beauty. Only by clearing the fog did I witness the innate energy of Life and only once connected to my personal God could I really come Alive and only when Alive could I offer my life.

Some might say to just start, to just try something, to have initiative, and to beat your fears. They would be right... But there's so much more that comes before this. Before you offer your true, authentic gifts, you must find what Truth and authenticity mean to you, you must discover yourself. Once you do, then, yes, go for it! Create! Give your whole heart, fail, learn, and create some more. But, first, focus on finding yourself.

This is how I came to coaching and why it fills me up. Our world focuses on the outcomes, the achievements, and the monetary success but not on the personal wellbeing of the people. My whole life I was a "high-achiever" but never felt Alive. Coaching became an opportunity to help people not only achieve and succeed but feel Alive while doing it. This book is the same. I don't want you to simply succeed but to feel the full spectrums of "umph" and "ahhh" of Life flowing through you. This requires tenacity, resilience, and courage.

The journey to creating your Art is like hiking up a mountain. It's challenging, you might get lost along the way, you're hungry and thirsty but don't have food or water. Walking your path and doing your work is hard. It requires owning your life completely. It means never acting like a victim of circumstance. It means listening to your intuition and doing what you must, no matter what.

In the hero's journey, the hero always tries to escape their calling before finally surrendering to the arduous adventure of finding their treasure within and gifting it to their village. Working at my local bakery was an example of running away from my path. When I quit, I thought I would be done running away from my path... But, well, I wasn't.

In August, I accepted a part-time job at an awesome startup called A Place Beyond (APB) in Arizona. After a month and a half of working on my coaching business, I moved across the country again for what once was my dream job. My job at APB was to lead outdoor trips, coach college students, and do business development. It was literally everything I could want from a job. I got to work with grounded and wise people, live in the midst of miles and miles of forest, and add to something I believed in. I made friends and built connections. I led workshops and helped people grow. I explored nature and had time for meditation, reading, and exercise. It was everything I ever wanted... Or so I thought.

As always, slowing down brought truth. Each morning, I hung between two ponderosa pines in my hammock to meditate. I watched the sun rise and shine through trunks and branches of great, old trees. I heard birds waking up and grounded into the present moment. As always, in presence was awareness. In my awareness, I felt an itch, an anxiety in my chest. In the stillness and peace, I was able to hear the soft whisper of my heart.

At first, I felt the whisper but didn't know what it meant. Then, over the weeks, I realized it was telling me to quit my dream job. I was shocked because, on paper, my job was perfect. I was surrounded by nature, living in healthy ways, and serving people I cared about. I loved my boss and my co-workers. I didn't want to leave, but I knew I had to. My Art was calling for me.

So, only two months after arriving, I left. When I told my boss, he asked me why and I said that it was just a knowing, that I somehow knew I needed to write a book. The job was exactly what I had always wanted, but it still didn't fit. I realized that If A Place Beyond wouldn't satisfy me, no job would. After I told everyone I was leaving, I wrote:

Announcing that I was leaving was probably one of the hardest things I've done. As I sat in the circle, laughing and having fun with all the wonderful people at APB, I started to frantically explore my mind for any potential way that I could stay. I wondered if I could make it work somehow. I desperately wanted to stay but as soon as I looked for a way not to, I felt the weight in my chest.

When I made the announcement, I didn't feel guilty. I knew it was the right choice, but I still shook and stumbled through my words.

On the same day I quit my job, I reneged on my acceptance from my corporate job that would start in January. If APB didn't do it for me, no way corporate would. For the first time in my entire life, I had no obligations. I had nothing I needed to do except feed myself and do my work. It was freeing beyond measure. It was terrifying. I wrote the next day:

I have no obligations. Everything that I do from now on is on my own terms. Whether I starve or eat, drive or stay put, work or play, rest or move... It's all up to me. It's an insane feeling to truly own my life. I'm filled with excitement and enthusiasm for this next phase, whatever it may throw at me.

I know that it won't be easy. I know that I will come up against demons and monsters like I've never seen, but I want to fight them, for this is my hero's journey, my venture into the unknown, my authentic path, and I am ready for it.

I quit both my jobs, don't have a home, have 700 dollars in my bank account, don't know where I'm driving next, am 18,000 dollars in debt, and feel good about it.

I'm overwhelmed because my decisions are those of an insane person. Holy shit, I don't even know how to say this. I feel empty and like I'm going to puke... But in a good way???

It was so overwhelming to have no path but my own. It meant that I had no direction except my own. Each decision in my life from this point forward had to come from me, and ideally from my connection to Life and to my personal God.

When I decided to work at APB, my intuition told me not to, but I let myself be convinced by friends and family because it seemed perfect. I had to go through this last experience to understand that ignoring my intuition won't ever, ever, ever work. When I quit, the responsibility of my whole life descended on me, overwhelmed me, terrified me, yet, it lit a fire to get moving, to do my work and so I did.

Homeless and with only the income from my coaching business, I left Arizona for adventure. From October 2020 to July 2021, I lived on couches, house sat, drove 7,000 miles, grew my coaching business, paid for coach training, moved to two new states, and wrote this book. It was not easy, but I felt more Alive than ever before.

After leaving APB, real depression was nowhere to be seen. I had days of melancholy, as we all do, but no major Dragons. Every time depression came, it was telling me to keep writing my book. When I stopped writing, depression came. When I wrote, it went away.

In committing to my Art, I found purpose. We each are born with purpose. Not *one* purpose, but *Purpose*. Not one Why, but Why. We are simply meant to be here, alive and breathing. You are here for a reason, even if you don't know what that reason is. The reason is not important. What is important is that there is a reason, always, for all of us.

We each have gifts and must, must, must give them. Without giving our gifts, we end the cycle of love and beauty. By coming alive through the spiritual journey, we allow Life to flow into us and offer us meaning but—and here is the crucial piece—we must not only let it flow in, but flow out, too. We are conduits for Life and Life's purpose is to Create, thus we must do as Life does and offer our lives to creation in the form of our Arts.

I couldn't not do my Art. I tried. I sought three jobs, moved across the country three times, and still couldn't escape my calling.

At the end of the spiritual healing journey isn't an end, but a beginning. As each of us heals and flourishes, we must offer our gifts to the world so it may flourish, too. A plant without flowers cannot spread beauty or its seeds. By doing our work from our healed cores, we spread sweet seeds of hope across the whole world. Put your heart to the Earth and listen for your calling. Have courage. Give your gift no matter what. The world needs you.

-23-

A REVOLUTION OF EVOLUTION

"Here is a test to find whether your mission on earth is finished: if you're alive, it isn't."
— RICHARD BACH

As I sat, writing this book in the winter mornings of New England, my candle burned down, and the sun came up. With the silence of the stars hanging in the sky, I toiled.

As I sat, editing this book in the summer evenings of Florida, my spirit lifted, and the sun fell. With the silence of the stars hanging in the sky, I toiled.

As a plant grows from seedling to sprout, so did I. As a tree grows from sprout to sapling, so did I. As the tree grows blossoms to pollinate Earth, so did I. This book is a fruition of my life's work so far. This book is the flowers of my magnolia tree, grown to share beauty and to spread its meaning.

I can't express how much it means to me to be writing these words, ending my story into the birth of our story.

As I've written this book, my story has twisted and turned, growing toward the sun like the crooked branches of my Magnolia. It carries in it my pain, mistakes, and vulnerabilities. I have shared my truest self with you, in all my imperfections. By doing so, I hope to also share the wonder and awe, the beauty and the meaning, in vulnerable authenticity. I hope to show you that there is hope and there are reasons to Live.

As I wrote this book, I shaped my past and healed wounds I didn't know I had. As I wrote the darkness from my childhood out of me, my past transformed into the reality that it actually was. The stories you've read represented the way I experienced life in memory, tainted by my suffering. As I wrote, other memories of happier times have taken over my heart and healed my history. I no longer regret my actions or resent myself or others for my pain or theirs. By letting the darkness out, I have made room for the light of my past to illuminate my way. There was joy in my past, just as there was pain. By opening to the pain, the joy shone.

Throughout my life, I experienced joy, I was just not aware of it. The joy is always around us. When we are suffering, we can't hold onto it. This is the worst part of Spiritual Depression: It reshapes our memories and gives us only darkness to hold onto. Healing is the process of reclaiming your own Life Light and your history in its fullness.

As we heal, by welcoming the gifts of our traumas and moving through our pains, we reshape our very histories. It is not just me, but all of us. As we collectively heal, we may reshape our collective history, recalling the ever-present Majesty of Life and Divine nature of humanity.

I began this book by talking about the end of the world and so I will end it by talking about the beginning.

In the beginning there was nothing. As far as we know, 13.7 billion years ago, out of nothing, came matter and energy. For the next 300 million years, nothing stirred. Then the first stars were born. For the next 8.9 billion years, stars pulled each other into galaxies and pulled rocks together into planets and asteroids. Then, about 4.5 billion years ago, a gigantic gas cloud pulled into itself to create our Galaxy. For hundreds of millions of years, there was only molten rock and fire; planets forming.

Then, rather miraculously, about 3.7 billion years ago, the first life form was born on our Earth. We still don't know how it happened. Over thousands of millions of years, life on Earth evolved. Many lifeforms were born and went extinct. Plants, animals, and everything in between lived, died, and evolved. Finally, very, very recently you were born. You are the product of almost 14 billion years of existence, and you are part of this grand unfolding of Life. We all are. Let that sink in. You are here on this Earth in the only perfect conditions we know of to allow Life to exist. You are *here*!

Everything, from snowflakes falling outside windows to piano music exists and we get to bear witness to it. We, humans, get to feel and hope and love and learn. We get to be curious and passionate. We get to feel pain and loss. We get to mourn and grieve. We get to pray and dance. We, the people of planet Earth, are Alive and we are powerful beyond measure.

Humans are undeniably special because we can ask ourselves questions: What is Life For? What are we For? Why Live?

We affect things differently than other animals, we experience life with intentionality, curiosity, and wonder. We change ourselves and our environments. We have taken evolution into our own hands, without knowing why we are evolving or what we are evolving toward and in doing so we have lost touch with our Life Source.

We escape the pain of Life because it scares us and by doing so we perpetuate our suffering and the suffering of Life. Where animals are a part of Nature, we are somehow capable of being outside it. Like the flower in my mushroom vision grew from the soil of Life but wasn't Life itself, we are capable of not being Life itself.

Humans are different because we can be between Life and God, between Heaven and Earth. But, really Heaven and Earth, Life, and God, The Divine and The Ordinary, are all the same. Heaven is Earth and Ordinary is Divine. Our perception of Life named God is Life itself. We have tried to be different because we have the capacity to choose. We have chosen to escape from the pain of Life into a sort of purgatory. We have escaped from the Divine into the desolation because numbness is easier than pain. We must reconnect to our source so that we can bring Life and God together once more. In order to live in Heaven, we must accept that Heaven is Earth.

Because Life is painful, we all have trauma and humanity has trauma. We hold ourselves at bay from the fullness of life to escape our experiences. In our shared trauma, we fight and hurt each other, we suffer and create machinations to perpetuate our suffering. We strive to move outside the realm of God, for fear of the pain we might find inside our suffering, inside Truth, inside Life. Humanity has lost its way.

But even so, in this cycle of terrible pain we have created for ourselves, the beauty of Life still abounds. Humanity, so far from Divine, is still surrounded by it, is it. We live in a world beyond our comprehension, where the simplest of serenities are the creations of 13.7 billion years of creation and 3.7 billion years of Life.

We, humans, have lost sight of this beauty, of this world in which we live. We have lost the Majesty and the Wonder around us. We have lost the meaning of God beneath the word. We have lost, in the muck of our own created distractions, the reality of what Is. We have grown to fear the welcoming nature of Life and the flow of Death.

These things are Natural. As each breath comes, it must go. To where, we don't know. As each person is born, so we must die and leave this Earth. To where, we don't know. Perhaps there is nothing after death for each individual, but after I die, life will sustain, and as I am a part of all Life and all Life is part of me, so shall I. My experience of living may die, but I shall sustain. We are mere mortals, living in a stream of immortal energy, circulating and compounding and growing. Life is circular and ever expanding. We are mortal beings without meaning, filled to the brim with more meaning and purpose and love than we know what to do with.

We belong here on Earth. You belong here on Earth. We, humans, are part of what is. And that is Divine.

But we have work to do. We may not accept the gifts of Life without giving in return our own gifts. It is the work of being human to heal yourself from your suffering by reconnecting to Life so you may return to Life your pain and your purpose. We offer our pain as teachings and Art and love to each other, to ourselves, to the world, and to Life, and in turn evolve into the future.

As humanity heals its collective trauma and pain, we will move from a world of suffering, a world in which people fight and kill, in which people refuse the innate beauty of each moment in favor of their own stagnation, in which people are afraid to die for dying is a lonely endeavor when done alone, toward a world of beauty, to a utopic Oneness with Life.

Death does not happen alone for those who are awake to Life. We are always together, one Life lived by the beings who are part of it. You are one such being. You are alive. You are a life. You are Life itself. Return to the flow.

When humans decide to ignore our own beauty, our own lives, our own capacity to give and to heal, we taint the entire flow with our suffering. When we refuse our own Divine Majesty, we enter into Spiritual Depression.

Why has the world suffered? Why do people hate? Why does racism exist? Why do people kill? Why do people do hurtful things? Why do people create horrors and perpetuate suffering?

It is because we do not know why we are here, because we have not healed and come together. Only those who have not healed are capable of such ugly emotions as hate. We suffer because we have been taught to by those who suffered before us. For thousands of years we have resisted the natural pains of life. The people who resisted it before we were born pass down to us stories that perpetuate this resistance. They taught us to be afraid of pain, to avoid going within ourselves, and to follow external guidance and dogmas instead of our own connection to Life.

But we are not meant to learn about God through the words of another. We must learn through the living of Life itself. We, each, are mystics, truly. We are here to bear witness to the manifestation of our own Gods, to live in accord with The Divine, to bring our True selves into Being.

A healed world is on its way. A revolution of humanity is called for. We must each break through our suffering like the sun clears fog and find the beauty beneath. We must be willing to love ourselves in our pain to find our Truth. We must open to Life and let Death flow through us. We must become One with All and Conduits for God. We must Live.

I call for revolution; for each of you to find in yourself your Truth, your calling, your pain, your gifts, your love, your faith, and your God. I call for you to let go of the shackles on your soul you hold to. I call for you to be here, in accord with your Truth and the beauty of life. I call for you to do your Work, your Art, your Creation, as we all must. Plant yourself in the Divine Life and offer your True Gifts. You matter!

As I call for revolution, so do I call for forgiveness. We, humans, have not been perfect. We, humans, have caused pain to each other, to the plants and animals around us, and to our own offspring. We have passed down and inherited generations of traumas and suffering through the created machinations of those who suffered before us. We have let our fears overwhelm us and keep us from the Glory of Life.

Here, I do call for us to forgive ourselves in order to begin anew. We acknowledge our imperfections and our mistakes. We own our responsibility as the stewards of our existence in the World around us. We shall do better. We shall heal ourselves, beginning in each of our hearts until the very Heart of Humanity has healed and we might find ourselves living in a bountiful, beautiful, spectacular world, welcomed into the future of All as One and One as All.

We, too, own our responsibility as pioneers, seeking to bring Life to the galaxies, to understand ourselves so we may understand Life itself, to surge into the desolation. We shall become one with Life again, I swear it, or we shall perish and Life shall go on without us. We must continue the grand revolution of evolution and change ourselves. We don't need gills or bigger guns, but self-love and more fun. We are Alive, people, part of Life. We are a bastion against the desolation. We are all the same. We must become a whole Life by first becoming our whole selves.

So, in the end, may there be a new beginning. The wheel revolves and ever evolves. As we each choose to live in accord with our callings and our Gods, may Life's Grand Calling be answered and may we rest in the bounty of Life.

Why Live? You tell me!

-24-

A LETTER TO MYSELF

*For a while I was looking for a person but I didn't
find them and after that I was looking for myself.
Now that I found me I'm back to exploring, which
is what I was doing in the first place before I was
doing anything else and I think I was supposed to
be exploring all along. Does that sound silly?*
– ERIN MORGENSTERN

Dear Faolan,

The last months of writing this book have not been easy.
You have experienced more resistance than ever before.
You have succumbed to your addictions and old demons.
You have fallen apart on the floor for hours at a time. Thank
you for not giving up on yourself and your Art. Thank you.

Never did I actually think that you would achieve your
dream of writing a book. This journey has been so hard for
us. I know. I can feel it...
You just had the biggest cry of your whole life as you wrote
those words and for good reasons.

Do you remember the pain you felt when you were a child, stuck in the tension between your parents? Do you remember when you escaped into porn and addiction and when you felt disgusted with your very existence? Do you remember staring at gray clouds your first year of college wondering what your purpose was? Do you remember sitting on the monkey bars having your first panic attack? Do you remember lying in bed in New Zealand finally coming alive for the first time by working through the muck? Do you remember standing at the crosswalk and deciding to keep living?

You could be dead. You chose not to be. You could still be living as an automaton in the numbness and fog. You chose not to. Thank you, from the bottom of my heart, thank you. I am beyond proud of you. You have overcome so much pain to be where you are, and at 23 years old no less.

I honestly can't believe where you are right now. You have the job of your dreams helping people come Alive to create their Art. You built your business from the ground up all by yourself and paid for your training by doing what you love. You wrote a whole book about your journey. Most importantly, you actually want to live.

Hear me when I say that it was not easy and that you've made it. Life from this point will never be the same. Writing these words, the ending to your first book, signifies a release of your old self. The tears that you let fall and the primal sounds that came out of you signify that letting go.

Last summer, you sat in the backyard by the lake arguing with your mom. You were so angry, but you took a deep breath and your anger transformed into Truth. You realized that you never thought you were good enough for her and you sobbed and she held you in her arms. You let her love enter you for the first time and you let her go.

Last February, on your 23rd birthday, you read the letter your dad wrote to you: "Happy birthday, son. Happy birthday, Faolan. I love you." Tears. You turned it over and found Shakespeare's sonnet 29. For the first time you fully accepted your father's love that has always been there for you and you sobbed and you let him go.

Today, as you wrote this letter to yourself, you found your purpose again in your art. You found authentic pride and a Majestic Gratitude for yourself, for God, and for Life. You accepted your whole self and your potential. You grieved your past self and you sobbed and you let yourself go.

This life is for you, by you, and I have complete faith that you will create what you are here to create. You are different, changed. With the final words of this book like a keystone in an arch, you close a chapter of your life and let go of your past to embrace your future.

Yesterday, you danced butt-naked in the pouring rain while accidentally tripping on mushrooms and smiled into the sky, your soul bright. This is the future for you, Faolan. This is your destiny. You may now accept it in all its brilliance and consider yourself worthy. You are worthy. You do deserve happiness, love, and anything else you ask of Life. Ask now, and you shall receive.

Of Life, all I ask for is to always feel fully Alive, in pain and in pleasure and all in between, I wish to feel it. Please, Life, God, Divine, whatever you are called, I ask for just this one thing. Please always let me feel Alive. I will do all I can to stay on my path, to face my fears, and to offer myself to You.

Faolan, you asked a question and I feel that I am finally ready to give you the answer... Why Live?

You live to be Alive. You live to feel each and every moment of sadness, grief, loss, pain, pleasure, pride, joy, exuberance, numbness, heartbreak, tiredness, and everything else. Each moment of your Life is a gift. Every single thing that you experience is a gift. Why Live? To be Alive! TO BE ALIVE!!!!

This Life is a gift! Your Life is a gift! You are a gift! There is no greater gift than to be, just as you are, right now, and always will be, Alive.

So, until this experience of living ends, I ask of thee: Do all you can to experience the fullness of each moment. Do not judge yourself for moments of weakness or pride yourself overly in moments of strength. Let yourself experience this life that you are lucky enough to live with the fullness of the Moon shining over rising tides and the wisteria blooming in the spring breeze.

Ultimately, the answer to your question will change and grow as you do. Never stop learning. Never stop reaching toward the sun and growing beyond where you were. Never stop being yourself. Shine bright, my love, and give yourself to Life with all you've got.

And now, the time has come for the final words.

I love, I am, I live... Life. Thank you for joining me along the way. I love you so, so much. Thank you, Faolan. Thank you, God. Thank you, Life. I Live.

Love,
Faolan

ACKNOWLEDGMENTS

It's fitting that I end this book with gratitude for everything that has brought me Life and for everyone who has helped me Live.

To Life itself, thank you for allowing us to live. I am eternally grateful.

To you, my dearest reader, thank you. You have truly made my life worth living. I wrote this book for myself initially but over time, I wrote it for you. You helped me wake up in the morning with a reason. I love you so much and I wish for you that all of Life graces your experience of living it. If you would like to get in touch, you can email me at hello@faolan.com. I would be overjoyed to hear from you. Thank you, thank you, thank you. I hope you got everything you were looking for and more from this book.

Mom, thank you for everything. There simply aren't words. I tried to write them but couldn't. You must settle for knowing that I love you endlessly, forever. I am so grateful for you. May you find the peace and space to finish this book and to love yourself as much as the rest of us do. ;)

Poppa, thank you. A few memories. Falling asleep within the first 10 pages of *The Sword of Shannara* 4 nights in a row. Hearing "we are never there, always here" and "it's all relative" countless times. Getting quizzed on long division in your blue truck. Hiking to the frog pond. You showed me eternities. Thank you.

Eliya, my love, thank you for shining your light for the last 10 years. Thank you for brightening the world and illuminating my path through the dark. You melted the ice around my heart. I will always, always be there for you. Never stop creating and moving your body.

Simona, your love is like the Sun itself. You push me to get on your level of love and always have. Sometimes I am amazed by how much you can love me, and I will always be grateful. If you need me, ever, just ask. I will come.

Judah, you are the cutest human being I know. The way you scrunch your forehead I have only ever seen myself and our dad do. Thank you for being pure love and for carving the way for our family to connect. I am excited to get to know you.

Jon, thank you for the sacrifices you have made to be my stepdad and an amazing father to your daughters. Thank you for your jokes and your wisdom. You may say that you are nothing, but truly, I believe you can be everything. Keep shining your light.

Emma, thank you for your humor and generosity. I want you to know that your resilience inspires me. You are such a powerful woman and human and your brain is sharp as a tack. I'm excited to learn more from you.

Grandma, let's just say that this book wouldn't exist without you. I wouldn't exist without you. You've been like a parent to me in so many ways. Thank you for picking up the phone, for staying up late with me, and for being my biggest supporter. You are an angel.

Grandpa, thank you for teaching me how to be a man. You were the first man I saw cry. I have learned so much from you about integrity, vulnerability, and tenacity. You inspire me with the dedication you have to all that is important to you. Here's to many more years of stupid jokes.

Yaya, you are a flower. I have loved to become not just your grandson but your friend. I want you to know that you've done a magnificent job of being the matriarch of our family. You are loving, compassionate, firm when needed, humorous, and light. Your smile is everything to me, I swear it.

To the rest of my family, thank you for making this life I'm living possible. Thank you for your generosity and your wisdom. Thank you for trusting me to carve my own path in life and for helping regardless of your own inclinations. I love you all.

To my friends along the way, thank you for making my life worth living. Thank you for holding space for me to not be okay and find okayness in my not okay. Thank you for being my rocks and for keeping me alive. Thank you for your patience throughout my many foolish learning experiences. Thank you for sharing innumerable experiences of joy with me. Thank you for the laughter. I hope for many more years of life together.

To my clients, you have made this life I live possible. You have taught me so much about myself and about life. You are the reason I wake up excited to "go to work" every day. Thank you for trusting me to accompany you to the many perilous edges of being human. Your courage, vulnerability, and dedication to growth inspire me every day. Thank you for empowering me to believe in myself and for giving me someone to write to. Hear me when I say, I love you like family and I would not be here if not for you.

To the people who have shared their homes with me as I wrote this book, thank you for your support. This book might not exist without you.

To those I have hurt, thank you for being strong enough to grow through the pain. Thank you for teaching me how to be better. Thank you for showing me my own pain and trauma. I'm sorry that you had to be part of my journey in these ways, but truly, I am grateful for you.

To the countless teachers, mentors, and coaches, who have believed in me over the years. This book wouldn't exist if not for you—know that. I am truly grateful that you saw something in me before I did. Thank you, forever.

Thank you, plants. From magic mushrooms and cannabis to my magnolia tree and the forests of my youth, you have been my greatest teachers.

Thank you, animals, you have graced my life and taught me to live as one with nature. Rattlesnake, I honor you. Thank you.

Finally, language, thank you for being beautifully insufficient at describing the magnitude of Life. Thank you to the craft of writing for giving my life meaning and helping me find light in the darkness. I hope to be in a very long relationship with you. Here's to many more books.

If you enjoyed this book, I have three earnest requests for you.

1. Please pass my book along or consider gifting another one to someone you think could benefit from reading it.

2. Send me an email with your thoughts or questions at hello@Faolan.com

3. Finally, it makes an immense difference to the success of my book to have honest reviews on Amazon, so if you could take a few minutes to review the book, that would be amazing!

Thank you and with love,
Faolan

Faolan Sugarman-Lash is on a mission to revolutionize mental and spiritual health by reimagining what gives life meaning. Faolan, when not writing, works directly with clients as a professional life coach. Trained by the Coaches Training Institute, he accompanies clients through their healing and creation journeys. Faolan is a world traveler and an avid supporter of the arts. You can almost always find him outside with a good book or on a hike. To stay up to date with his adventures or to learn more, follow Faolan on Instagram (@Faolan) or subscribe to his newsletter at Faolan.com.